⁐ MEZE ⁐

SMALL BITES, BIG FLAVORS
from the GREEK TABLE

BY **ROSEMARY BARRON** ∽ PHOTOGRAPHS BY **DAVID ROTH**

CHRONICLE BOOKS
SAN FRANCISCO

Library of Congress Cataloging-in-Publication Data available.

ISBN 0-8118-3148-5

PRINTED IN CHINA

PROP STYLING by **KATE MARTINDALE**
FOOD STYLING by **CHRISTINE MASTERSON**
DESIGNED by **AISHA BURNES**
PHOTOGRAPHY ASSISTANCE by **THOMAS EDWARDS**

DISTRIBUTED in CANADA by **RAINCOAST BOOKS**
9050 SHAUGHNESSY STREET, VANCOUVER, BC V6P 6E5

10 9 8 7 6 5 4 3 2 1

CHRONICLE BOOKS LLC
85 SECOND STREET, SAN FRANCISCO, CALIFORNIA 94105
www.chroniclebooks.com

ACKNOWLEDGEMENT
My heartfelt thanks to Pat Herbert, whose skills and good sense give
me confidence. I'd also like to thank Lidia and Sotiris Kitrilakis, Jeanne
Quan, Terence Murphy, Anne Dolamore, Gloria Capel, Angel Stoyanof,
Meredith Pillon, and Geraldene Holt, who all generously gave me their
time and expertise; Cordell Barron, for his honest opinions; editor, Amy
Treadwell; photographer, David Roth; designer, Aisha Burnes; food
stylist, Christine Masterson; art director, Azi Rad; Thomas Edwards and
Kate Martindale. Special thanks always to Bill LeBlond and Fred Hill.

INTRODUCTION

Mezes are one of the most enjoyable and companionable aspects of Greek life, served everywhere from the humblest beachfront café to the most elegant city hotel. An approximate translation of the word is "appetizers," a wholly inadequate term to express the variety, vitality, and sensual pleasure of the meze table, or its integral place in the national culture.

Mezes are the embodiment of living, continuing tradition; in them, modern Greeks experience and savor the flavors, textures, and ingredients that excited and intrigued their forebears in the ancient classical world. My own interest in the Greek food past began when I took part in archaeological digs on Crete in the 1960s. I can still remember being amazed that I was eating, quite naturally, and in the same manner, foods of which we were uncovering evidence of thousands of years earlier: wild greens, grains, fish, game, wines, olives, and olive oil.

The meze table originated in that long-ago past and began as common sense. The ancients discovered, no doubt through bitter experience, that drinking on an empty stomach was bad news and that alcohol's less-pleasing effects could be avoided or reduced by the simple expedient of eating morsels of food while drinking. Gradually, this practical custom was elevated to the status of a social ritual, making it culturally unacceptable to drink without eating, and the snacks-with-drinks habit developed into a new way of eating. Today, the tradition and culture of the meze table is woven into the fabric of Greek life; what began as a precaution is now a framework for social interaction and the unhurried enjoyment of fresh, seasonal, and intensely flavored food.

Step back twenty-five hundred years and imagine yourself at a social gathering of philosophers in the ancient Greek world. This is a world where food and eating are considered an art and analyzed with scientific precision. The table spread before you, according to a description Plato gives, offers platters of radishes, olives, beans, green vegetables, figs, cheese, garbanzo beans, and myrtle. In other words, a balanced assembly of fresh and preserved foods, sweet and savory, melting or crunchy, with flavors ranging from delicate to dramatic. Now, think yourself forward to a family birthday party in modern Greece, and amazingly, the table displays exactly the same principle of contrasts and many of the same components: fresh and preserved vegetables; tiny savory pies; crunchy nuts; salads; nutty, chewy bread; tiny patties of meat or fish; crumbly cheese; smoked and dried meats; mouthfuls of fish, shellfish, octopus, or smoked eel; and fresh or dried fruit.

The meze table can have as few as five dishes or as many as twenty-five, and they may be chosen according to region or season. In a simple country taverna, mezes may be just a few plump olives, two or three chunks of refreshing tomato or cucumber, a pickled vegetable, and some crumbly fresh cheese; in the mountains they may be country ham, sausage, or roasted meat scented with pungent herbs, or puréed vegetables or pulses; on the coast, mezes exploit the sea's plenty with seafood fritters, pieces of boiled octopus or baby squid, small fish grilled or fried, little clams, or spiny sea urchins from which you scoop the coral roe.

In spring, there will be the first fava beans, almonds, and walnuts to nibble raw; in summer, luscious, deeply flavored tomatoes, stuffed small eggplants, zucchini, and sweet bell peppers; in autumn and winter, comforting dishes based on dried beans, and mellow roasted vegetables. Throughout Greece, the visitor encounters regional mezes, expressing the continuing culinary influences of the Byzantine empire or the Turkish and Venetian occupations. Or, mezes may simply express the local character of a town or village: dishes made from what's seasonally available in gardens, fields, markets, and from the pantry.

However basic or grand the meze table, the overriding principle is the same: dishes of distinctive or unusual flavor skillfully selected to complement or contrast with each other. There should be immediate visual appeal, followed by satisfaction and surprise in taste and texture.

The ancients either were wiser than we give them credit for, or they had an unerring instinct for food that was both flavorful and nutritionally correct. The modern Greek diet is more varied than theirs, but it is still rich in olive oil, fresh vegetables, nuts and seeds, salads and wild greens, pulses, fish, and lean meats (often grilled), and low on dairy foods and saturated fats.

Just to give a few examples: We now know from modern research that the wild greens Greeks love so much are rich sources of vitamins and minerals; that seaside meze treats such as sardines, bonito, or tuna are important sources of healthful fish oils; that a diet combining garlic and olive oil can help reduce the incidence of heart disease; that honey is packed with vitamins and maybe even a healing "ingredient X"; that pulses are an excellent source of protein; and that dried fruits are high in mineral content and energy-giving carbohydrates.

The more health-conscious among us may try to incorporate some of these healthful elements into our diets, but we tend to do it half-heartedly or with uninspired dedication, or we resort to dietary supplements. The glory of Greek meze cooking is that it offers these essential and natural nutrients in a form that's attractive, stimulating, and enjoyable. Greeks don't eat mezes because they are good for them, but because they taste wonderful and because the whole meze table experience has a relaxing, sensual, and even spiritual dimension. Following their example, we can make the food wisdom of the ancients work for us, too.

But does the meze table have any relevance for our modern lifestyle, and is it hard work? To the first, I would answer emphatically "yes" and to the second, a resounding "no"! Mezes are very well suited to the way we live now and, for the most part, take no longer to prepare than a casserole.

Above all, the Greek meze table shows us how to slow down; how to enjoy flavor, texture, and diversity; how to make the most of simple preparations and seasonal goodness. Best of all, mezes are supremely sociable; this is food to share with other people in an atmosphere of friendship and community.

As you cook your way through this book you'll find food for any occasion, from picnics and al fresco eating to late suppers or quick and simple lunches, healthy snacks for cocktail parties or in-between meals, and exciting first courses. Many of the dishes can be prepared ahead of time and the quantities doubled or tripled for large parties. You'll also find that you are making better use of local foods and buying your ingredients fresh and in season— to your nutritional and financial benefit.

A meze serving is, at the most, two mouthfuls. You can serve one or two different meze dishes as a first course, or five or six per person as a light meal. For a cocktail party, circulate four or five easy-to-eat kinds of mezes, and for a spectacular buffet provide a careful selection of twelve to sixteen varieties. Arrange your meze table to exploit all the variations in color and texture: tiny golden pies next to a tomato salad; a creamy vegetable purée near a dish of glossy black olives; little meat patties, garnished with bright lemon wedges, next to salad greens. And if you're serving mezes as an hors d'oeuvre, or with drinks, be sure to keep the quantities small, otherwise appetites will be satisfied rather than stimulated. These little dishes are called *mezedakia* (small mezes).

THE MEZE PANTRY

The key to assembling an authentic Greek meze table is to make sure that your basic building blocks—olive oil, olives, yogurt, cheese, herbs, vegetables, fish, and meat—are of top quality. Preparing attractive mezes does not mean hours in the kitchen working on fussy preparations and mastering complicated cooking techniques. It does mean finding the best suppliers, choosing food in prime condition, and occasionally preparing a few Greek pantry basics.

The staples of the meze table are convenience foods in the best sense of the term: foods that make good cooking easier and quicker. With a selection of these at hand, you can compose attractive, healthy appetizers and light meals in minutes. All capture the authentic aromas, tastes, and textures of traditional mezes.

With a few foods always at hand in your pantry and refrigerator/freezer, plus others that you can grow or buy, you can compose a tempting, imaginative meze table even on days when you have little time to shop.

FROM THE PANTRY

BOTTLED ROASTED RED BELL PEPPERS

CANNED ARTICHOKE HEARTS

CAPERS AND CAPER LEAVES: *salt-packed*

DRIED FRUIT: *currants; small dark raisins; figs; prunes*

DRIED HERBS: *bay leaves, whole and ground; marjorum; mint; rigani (Greek oregano), small branches and leaves; rosemary; sage; thyme; winter savory*

DRIED PULSES: *garbanzo beans (chickpeas); white beans (great northerns, cannellini); green lentils; brown lentils; yellow split peas; butter (large lima) beans*

HONEY: *hymettus; orange blossom*

NUTS: *whole unblanched almonds; walnuts in the shell; pine nuts; unsalted pistachio nuts; hazelnuts (filberts)*

OLIVE OIL: *extra-virgin; kalamata extra-virgin*

OLIVES: *brine-cured; young and green; salt-cured; plump and fleshy; sweet and tiny*

PICKLES: *toursi (traditionally prepared peppers and vegetables, from northern Greece or Turkey); dill-spiced tiny cucumbers*

PRESERVED FISH: *salted anchovies; sardines packed in olive oil or brine; tuna packed in olive oil; oil-cured bonito (lakertha); sun-dried mackerel or octopus; smoked eel; avgotaracho (pressed mullet roe)*

PRESERVED GRAPE LEAVES

PRESERVED LEMONS

SEA SALT: *fine and coarse*

SEEDS: *melon; pumpkin; sesame; sunflower*

SPICES: *allspice, ground; cinnamon, sticks and ground; coriander seeds, whole and ground; cumin, whole and ground; black peppercorns; fennel, whole; sumac, ground; paprika, ground*

SUN-DRIED TOMATOES: *packed in olive oil*

VINEGAR: *aged red wine; red wine; balsamic*

FROM THE REFRIGERATOR OR FREEZER

CHEESES: *feta in brine; aged graviera; aged kephalotyri, Italian pecorino, or parmesan; manouri or good-quality mozzarella*

FRESH OR FROZEN FILO SHEETS: *(you can store fresh filo for up to 2 days, frozen filo for up to 4 weeks)*

YOGURT

QUICK & SIMPLE DISHES

Now, you're ready to compose any of the following quick and simple dishes. Serve as part of a meze table together with recipes from other chapters in this book, or as a quick snack or first course:

- Drain canned SARDINES and sprinkle with coarse sea salt, freshly ground pepper, a few drops of lemon juice, minced fresh flat-leaf parsley, and extra-virgin olive oil.

- Drain canned TUNA, separate into chunks, and cover with thinly sliced red onion; sprinkle with sumac, extra-virgin olive oil, and coarse sea salt.

- Lay small pieces of SMOKED EEL alongside trimmed green onions and slices of cold cooked potatoes in Olive Oil & Red Wine Vinegar Sauce (see page 16).

- Sprinkle SUN-DRIED MACKEREL with red wine vinegar, extra-virgin olive oil, and dried Greek oregano or rigani, and serve with black olives and slices of pickled or fresh cucumber.

- Lightly toast skin-on ALMONDS and serve with cucumber chunks, radishes, olives, tomato wedges, feta cheese, and quartered dried figs.

- Roast CHESTNUTS in a fire or on a grill, sprinkle with sea salt, and serve with Amfissa olives and mixed salad greens.

- Heap skinned toasted HAZELNUTS, ALMONDS, or WALNUTS (or a mixture) on a small platter and pour hymettus honey over; serve with coffee and/or slices of fresh fruit and manouri cheese or Yogurt Cheese (see page 18).

- Mix cooked WHITE BEANS with Olive Oil & Red Wine Vinegar Sauce (see page 16), chopped green onion, and capers and/or caper leaves; sprinkle with feta cheese, paprika, and fresh thyme.

- Combine cooked LENTILS, minced shallot, finely diced preserved lemon, extra-virgin olive oil, and plenty of watercress sprigs.

- Combine cooked GARBANZO BEANS with Olive Oil & Lemon Juice Sauce (see page 16) and plenty of minced chives and young arugula or purslane.

- Arrange ROASTED RED BELL PEPPER strips on a plate with anchovy fillets, capers, and Elitses or niçoise olives; sprinkle with minced fennel fronds and extra-virgin olive oil.

- Sprinkle FETA CHEESE with dried Greek oregano or rigani and extra-virgin olive oil; serve with olives and cherry tomatoes or capers, caper leaves, fresh radishes, and cucumber chunks.

- Serve OYSTERS on the half shell with Olive Oil & Red Wine Vinegar Sauce (see page 16), mixed with minced shallot and fresh flat-leaf parsley.

- Sauté SHRIMP in olive oil, drizzle with lemon juice, and serve cold, sprinkled with dried Greek oregano or rigani, coarse sea salt, and freshly ground pepper.

- Combine large flakes or small pieces of leftover cooked WHITE FISH with Olive Oil & Lemon Juice Sauce (see page 16), coarse sea salt, freshly ground pepper, and minced mixed fresh herbs; serve with olives.

- Cut ROMAINE LETTUCE into thin slices, sprinkle with fresh lemon juice, extra-virgin olive oil, and coarse sea salt, and mix with slivered green onion and minced fresh flat-leaf parsley.

- Steam tiny whole CARROTS or small CAULIFLOWER FLORETS and combine with Olive Oil & Lemon Juice Sauce (see page 16) and minced fresh cilantro; serve cold.

- Combine diced cooked TURNIP with a few currants, dried Greek oregano or rigani, and Olive Oil & Red Wine Vinegar Sauce (see page 16); serve with slices of ham.

- Mix lightly cooked GREEN BEANS with Olive Oil & Red Wine Vinegar Sauce (see page 16) and sprinkle with dried Greek oregano or rigani, coarse sea salt, and minced fresh flat-leaf parsley.

- Fry EGGPLANT or ZUCCHINI slices in olive oil and sprinkle with a few drops of red wine vinegar; serve with yogurt and Elitses or niçoise olives.

- Combine diced CUCUMBER with chopped red onion, thinly sliced radishes, and minced fresh flat-leaf parsley, and sprinkle with lemon juice, olive oil, and a little sumac.

- Mix equal quantities of finely diced cooked BEETS, CARROTS, and POTATOES with homemade or good-quality commercial mayonnaise; sprinkle with capers.

- Combine equal quantities of SHREDDED CABBAGE and CARROT with thinly sliced green onions and minced fresh flat-leaf parsley; stir in Olive Oil & Lemon Juice Sauce (see page 16).

- Serve sliced ripe TOMATOES with thasos or salt-cured black olives, paper-thin slices of red onion, and minced fresh marjoram, or with arugula torn into bite-sized pieces, Elitses or niçoise olives, and crumbled feta cheese; sprinkle with extra-virgin olive oil and coarsely ground pepper.

AROMATIC OLIVES

Steeping brine-cured olives in a strongly flavored marinade mellows their piquancy. This version is a Peloponnese family recipe, and the marinade flavors—lemon, dried Greek oregano or rigani, capers—are feisty. Any leftover marinade can be used later as a salad dressing.

For a simple meze table with a wide appeal, serve with Little Cheeses in Olive Oil (page 19), Passatempo (page 22), radishes, cucumber sticks, and sliced sweet tomatoes. These olives are also good with grills, preserved meats, or fish or bean dishes.

Makes 8 meze servings

1 teaspoon grated organic lemon zest

1 tablespoon salt-packed capers, soaked, rinsed, and patted dry (see page 118)

1 salt-packed anchovy fillet, rinsed, soaked, and patted dry (see page 118)

1 tablespoon dried Greek oregano or rigani

½ small clove garlic, minced (optional)

¼ cup extra-virgin olive oil

1 cup mixed Greek olives, pitted

¼ teaspoon coarsely ground pepper, or to taste

4 bay leaves

¼ cup minced fresh herbs such as flat-leaf parsley, cilantro, fennel fronds, chervil, rosemary, or thyme, or a mixture

In a mortar or small bowl, combine the lemon zest, capers, anchovy, oregano, and garlic, if using. Pound with a pestle or wooden spoon until well mashed. Stir in the olive oil and set aside.

Leave the olives whole or cut them into quarters or smaller. In a medium bowl, combine the olives, pepper, bay leaves, and anchovy mixture. Stir to blend with a wooden spoon. Cover and set aside at room temperature for at least 1 hour or up to 3 hours.

To serve, stir in the fresh herbs and transfer to a serving dish or bowl.

TWO OLIVE OIL SAUCES

Here are two quick and versatile olive oil sauces to use on any meze occasion, one made with red wine vinegar (lathoxsitho), the other with lemon juice (latholemono). Sometimes garlic, mustard, and/or herbs are added to either sauce, and lathoxsitho is occasionally sweetened with honey. The formula is simple: 1 part acid to 4 to 5 parts olive oil, or to your taste. Both sauces make delicious salad dressings for fresh, steamed, boiled, or roasted vegetables, and add interest to grilled fish, seafood, or meats. Used as a marinade for vegetables, fish, meats, and variety meats, they tenderize and flavor.

Serve mezes flavored with red wine vinegar with a bold red wine or tsipouro, and those flavored with lemon juice with ouzo, retsina, or a distinctive white wine.

OLIVE OIL & RED WINE VINEGAR SAUCE (LATHOXSITHO)

Makes ½ cup

1 tablespoon aged red wine vinegar

¼ to ½ teaspoon Hymettus or other strongly flavored honey, or to taste

½ teaspoon Meaux or other mild mustard (optional)

¼ to ⅓ cup extra-virgin olive oil, or to taste

1 teaspoon dried thyme or Greek oregano, crumbled, or 2 teaspoons minced fresh marjoram or herb of choice

In a medium bowl, combine the vinegar, honey, and mustard, if using. Whisk in the olive oil and stir in the herbs.

OLIVE OIL & LEMON JUICE SAUCE (LATHOLEMONO)

Makes ⅔ cup

Juice of ½ a small lemon

Large pinch of dry mustard (optional)

1 small clove garlic, minced (optional)

¼ to ⅓ cup extra-virgin olive oil, or to taste

1 teaspoon dried Greek oregano or rigani, crumbled, or 2 teaspoons minced fresh marjoram or herb of choice (optional)

¼ cup minced fresh flat-leaf parsley (optional)

In a medium bowl, combine the lemon juice, and mustard and garlic, if using. Whisk in the olive oil and stir in the herbs, if using.

HOMEMADE YOGURT

Thick, creamy yogurt and robust, tangy cheeses take pride of place on the meze table. The best Greek yogurt is made from sheep's milk, but you can make good yogurt at home from cow's milk. You don't need complicated equipment, and your effort will be richly rewarded by the freshness and authenticity of flavor you achieve. I have also included here yogurt cheese, a successful substitute for the fresh Greek country cheeses that cannot be found outside Greece.

Making yogurt is simple. You just need good-quality fresh milk and cream, a few tablespoons of commercial natural plain yogurt (without gelatin or stabilizer), spotless utensils, and a warm, draft-free spot. If your yogurt fails to set, the incubating spot is too cool and the temperature fluctuating; if it curdles, it has been kept at too warm a temperature or has been left incubating for too long.

Village Yogurt is a creamier, thickened version of homemade yogurt modeled on a magnificent sheep's milk yogurt I found in the Cretan village of Vrisses some years ago. I've yet to find a yogurt that tastes better than that village version, but I think my recipe captures some of its ultracreamy quality. The flavor of your yogurt will depend on the length of incubating time (the flavor intensifies the longer it sits), the age and character of your culture or starter, and the type and freshness of the milk you use.

Makes 4 cups

3 cups organic whole milk

1 cup half-and-half or light cream

3 tablespoons plain natural yogurt

In a medium, heavy saucepan, combine the milk and cream. Bring to a bare simmer over low heat. Pour into a bowl and let cool to 105 to 110°F, or to the moment you can comfortably leave your little finger in the milk for a count of 5. Skin will form on the surface (this makes a special treat later, with honey); push part of it to one side and spoon the yogurt into the milk.

For yogurt with a textured crust, leave uncovered, or cover with a tea towel, for 8 to 12 hours in a warm, draft-free spot (such as on top of the refrigerator or on a shelf above the stove); for yogurt without a crust, cover the bowl with a plate or lid before incubating. On a very cold day, wrap the bowl in a towel.

Remove the yogurt from the incubating spot and let cool to room temperature. Cover the bowl with a plate or plastic wrap and refrigerate for up to 3 days.

VILLAGE YOGURT: Set a sieve over a bowl and line with 2 layers of cheesecloth; cut the pieces large enough to hang over the sides of the sieve. Pour in the freshly made yogurt, pull up the sides of the cheesecloth, and tie together to make a bag. Hang the bag from a shelf or a faucet over the bowl for 2 hours to drain (don't refrigerate; the cold temperature will firm but not thicken the yogurt).

To store, scoop out the now-thickened yogurt into a bowl or container, cover with a plate or lid, and refrigerate for up to 3 days. Refrigerate the whey (the liquid remaining in the bowl), too, and use within 2 days in breads, soups, or milkshakes.

YOGURT CHEESE

You may question whether it's worth making your own cheese, to which I would reply that yogurt cheese is simple to make, and it's a surefire way to make your meze table authentically Greek.

This cheese is soft and white, with a refreshing tangy taste. Accompanied with olives, it's a seductive appetizer; with fresh ripe fruit, an aromatic honey, and a sweet Samos Nectar wine, it's a delicious sweet.

Makes 1¼ cups

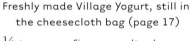

Freshly made Village Yogurt, still in the cheesecloth bag (page 17)

¼ teaspoon fine sea salt, plus more to taste

Extra-virgin olive oil to taste

Freshly ground pepper to taste

Minced fresh herbs to taste

Set a sieve or colander over a bowl and place the yogurt, still in its cheesecloth bag, in it. Open the bag, gently mix in the ¼ teaspoon salt with a wooden spoon, and replace the cheesecloth over the top of the yogurt. Set a small plate on top, weight with a can of food, and set aside for 2 hours in a cool, out-of-the-way spot to drain. Transfer the sieve or colander, yogurt, and bowl to the refrigerator and leave overnight, with the weight still in place. (Use the whey in soups or bread making; refrigerate no longer than 2 days.)

Remove the bag from the sieve and pat the cheesecloth dry with paper towels. Store the wrapped cheese in a bowl or container, tightly covered with plastic wrap or a lid, in the refrigerator for up to 3 days.

To serve, unfold the top of the cheesecloth bag, invert a small platter over the cheese, and turn the cheese out; peel off the cheesecloth. Sprinkle with olive oil, salt, pepper, and herbs.

LITTLE CHEESES IN OLIVE OIL

These creamy, bay-scented cheeses make perfect partners for fresh fruits such as figs, melon, or peaches. If you store them just a few days, the flavor is delicately sweet; leave them longer, and the taste mellows and deepens.

I like to serve the mellower cheeses with bean dishes, fresh fava beans, grilled eggplant, or liver, or as part of a meze platter, with olives. For optimum flavor, use a young, good-quality olive oil (any leftover oil can be used in salad dressing).

Makes 8 cheeses

> Yogurt Cheese, no more than 2 days old (page 18)
>
> 8 large bay leaves, or as needed
>
> Extra-virgin olive oil to cover
>
> Coarse sea salt and freshly ground pepper to taste
>
> Minced fresh flat-leaf parsley, or fresh or dried herb of choice

Carefully break the cheese into 8 portions and form each portion into a ball; gently press between your palms to slightly flatten, and smooth the edges with your fingers. Arrange the cheeses in a single layer in a shallow bowl. Tightly cover the dish with plastic wrap (but avoid crushing the cheeses) and refrigerate overnight.

Reserve the 2 longest bay leaves. Lay 2 bay leaves on the bottom of the jar and arrange a single layer of cheeses on top. Cover with 1 or 2 bay leaves, then add a second layer of cheeses; continue until you have layered all the cheeses and bay leaves. (The bay leaves help keep the cheeses separate during storage.) Place the 2 reserved bay leaves on top of the cheeses. Gently push the ends of the leaves down inside the jar. If the leaves are not long enough to reach the sides of the jar, to act as a lid to keep the cheeses in place, gently wedge 2 wooden skewers on top of them. Pour in olive oil to cover the cheeses; the long bay leaves or skewers will keep them immersed. Tightly cover the jar with a lid or 2 layers of waxed paper secured under a lid, and store in a cool, dark place for at least 2 weeks or up to 2 months.

To serve, remove the cheeses from the jar with a small rubber spatula and arrange on a small platter or on individual plates. Sprinkle with salt, pepper, and parsley. Drizzle a little olive oil from the jar. To serve with fruit, hold the cheese over the jar for a few seconds to let excessive olive oil drip back into the jar, and garnish with 1 or 2 of the bay leaves. If using only 1 or 2 cheeses, make sure that the remaining cheeses are covered with olive oil before storing longer.

VARIATION: For a traditional island flavor, cover the cheeses with herbs before storing in olive oil. Spread 2 tablespoons dried Greek oregano or rigani, marjoram, winter savory, or thyme leaves on a plate and gently press each cheese into the herb before storing; layer with bay leaves and use 2 sprigs of the flavoring herb, or wooden skewers, to keep the cheeses immersed.

MEZEDAKIA

In Greece, drinks are always served with tiny tidbits known as *mezedakia*. These can be simple offerings of olives and bread or dishes of roasted garbanzo beans, sunflower seeds, or almonds, or stunningly elaborate platters of several skillfully chosen dishes.

The role of mezedakia is to stimulate the taste buds and appetite, to intrigue, lure, and tantalize, first by appearance and then by taste. A successful mezedakia platter offers salty snacks (olives, capers, preserved fish), something refreshing or juicy (cucumber, melon or tomato wedges, radishes, wild artichokes, fresh fava beans), food to crunch (almonds, walnuts, pistachio nuts, melon seeds, meze breads), and a sweet treat (figs or plump raisins). Each element—in color, texture, and taste—works with others in an aesthetic combination that both surprises and delights.

Mezedakia vary according to season and location. In a village blessed with walnut trees, you may be served young, soft-shelled walnuts, or plump nuts pickled or honey-steeped. At a harborside café, limpets, razor shells, sea anemones, sea violets, and sea urchins are often the mezedakia specialty.

Mezedakia platters can be a brilliant substitute for the bland cocktail snacks and potato chips we all nibble rather absentmindedly at cocktail parties. Refreshingly different, quick to make, and nutritious, mezedakia are also perfect for a relaxing evening with friends over a bottle of wine. They are a stimulating talking point, and I find my guests take a lively interest in the history and composition of these enticing little dishes. Many mezedakia also make excellent first courses.

For a mezedakia platter to work well, it's important to balance the intense flavors and different textures cleverly. Here are some typically Greek mezedakia platters. With a little practice, you'll quickly be composing innovative creations of your own.

PASSATEMPO

Passatempo *means "passing the time," and for Greeks the best way to do this is to chat with friends over a glass of ouzo, tsipouro, or wine. Since, by ancient custom, they never drink without eating, these conversations are punctuated by nibbles of nuts, dried fruits, or sunflower or melon seeds. Over the centuries, the name of this civilized pastime has transferred to the snacks, and to modern Greeks passatempo means crunchy mouthfuls to accompany alcoholic drinks.*

For us, walnuts, sunflower seeds, toasted hazelnuts or chestnuts, and raisins mixed with aniseed or fennel seeds make wonderful cocktail nibbles. Add radishes, olives, and chunks of feta cheese and cucumber for a classic meze table. For a more ambitious selection, add the following:

Makes 8 meze servings

1 cup unblanched almonds

3 tablespoons fresh lemon juice

8 plump dried figs, trimmed and quartered lengthwise

1 tablespoon plus 1 teaspoon red wine vinegar

2 tablespoons water

1 cup pistachio nuts, preferably unsalted

½ cup pine nuts

2 tablespoons coarse sea salt

2 tablespoons sesame seeds

¼ cup dried currants

In a small bowl, combine the almonds and 2 tablespoons of the lemon juice. Mix well with a wooden spoon and set aside for 15 minutes.

In another small bowl, combine the figs, the 1 tablespoon vinegar, and water; stir to coat. Set aside for 15 minutes.

Preheat the oven to 325°F. Arrange two shelves close to the top of the oven.

Spread the almonds in one layer at one end of a jellyroll pan, and spread the pistachios at the other end. In the same fashion, spread the pine nuts and figs in a second pan. Sprinkle the almonds with 1 tablespoon of the salt and put this pan on the top shelf. After 5 minutes, remove the pan and sprinkle the pistachios with the remaining 1 tablespoon lemon juice and ½ tablespoon salt. Return to the oven and toast 10 minutes longer, or until the almonds are crisp and beginning to brown.

Meanwhile, sprinkle the pine nuts with the remaining ½ tablespoon salt and the figs with the sesame seeds. Place the pan on the lower oven shelf and bake for 10 minutes; roll the nuts in the salt once or twice during baking.

Put the almonds, pistachios, pine nuts, and figs in separate bowls. Sprinkle the currants with the 1 teaspoon vinegar and add to the pine nuts. Serve with other mezedakia (see headnote).

BRINE-CURED BONITO WITH CAPERS

When you need a quick-to-make appetizer with a racy flavor, this fits the bill perfectly. A traditional meze with a long history, brine-cured bonito has a salty depth of meaty flavor and is rich in healthful fish oils. You can find it in Greek and Middle Eastern stores; ask for lakertha (which is brine-cured in wooden barrels; see page 118), or imported Greek or Italian bonito or tuna packed in olive oil. At home, sprinkle thin strips of fish with sharp lemon juice and serve with a refreshing dill and cucumber dressing and a glass of ouzo (see page 126).

Makes 8 meze servings

½ English (hothouse) cucumber, peeled

½ tablespoon coarse sea salt

2 tablespoons white wine vinegar

4 ounces lakertha (brine-cured bonito) or oil-packed bonito or tuna

Coarsely ground pepper to taste

1 tablespoon fresh lemon juice

2 tablespoons extra-virgin olive oil

2 tablespoons minced fresh dill or flat-leaf parsley, plus dill or flat-leaf parsley sprigs for garnish

½ teaspoon honey

1 tablespoon salt-packed small capers, soaked, rinsed, and patted dry (see page 118)

8 Elitses or niçoise olives

With a mandoline or knife, cut the cucumber into matchsticks, or use the julienne blade on a food processor. Sprinkle with the salt and set aside for 1 hour.

Dip a paper towel in the vinegar and wipe the bonito (the vinegar removes the strong-flavored brine). Rinse well; dry with more paper towels. With a filleting knife or a sharp, thin-bladed knife, cut the fish into thin crosswise slices, then into ⅛-inch-wide strips. Arrange in a crisscross pattern on one side of a platter and sprinkle with the pepper, ½ tablespoon of the lemon juice, 1 tablespoon of the olive oil, and 1 tablespoon of the minced dill or parsley.

In a small bowl, combine the honey and remaining lemon juice. Stir to mix, then whisk in the remaining 1 tablespoon olive oil. With your hand, squeeze the cucumber pieces to rid them of some of their water. Add them to the sauce with the remaining minced dill or parsley; stir to mix. Arrange on the platter alongside the fish, and heap capers and olives either side. Garnish with dill or parsley sprigs.

VARIATION: In place of bonito or tuna, try smoked mackerel or canned sardines (packed in olive oil), but don't wipe either of these fish with vinegar.

TRADITIONAL HAM "KATAIFI"

Most of us are familiar with sweet kataifi: honey-drenched treats of shredded filo pastry wrapped around a filling of nuts and spices. Here the kataifi-wrap principle is adapted to enclose fresh sheep cheese in paper-thin slices of cured ham. If you can find it, use traditional Greek pastourmas, or substitute speck or prosciutto. Greek manouri is the traditional cheese, but a good-quality mozzarella or goat cheese also works well. Try not to economize on ingredients; this simple dish relies on top-grade ham and cheese for the best flavor and texture.

Makes 8 meze servings

12 ounces manouri, mozzarella, or fresh white goat cheese, cut into 8 neat fingers

8 paper-thin slices pastourmas, speck, or prosciutto, trimmed of all fat

24 small sprigs mâche, samphire, or mixed salad greens

16 Elitses or niçoise olives

Coarsely ground pepper to taste

Extra-virgin olive oil for sprinkling

Coarse sea salt to taste (optional)

Wrap each piece of cheese in 1 slice of ham (it doesn't matter if some cheese remains exposed). Arrange on a platter or on individual plates, with the greens and olives alongside. Sprinkle the kataifi with pepper and the greens with olive oil and salt, if desired.

PIQUANT ALMOND FIGS

Assembled in minutes from pantry ingredients, this meze is a lifesaver when you need a tasty appetizer in a hurry. The firm fruit and crunchy nuts combine with a sweet-sour dressing to create an explosion of taste and textures. It looks good, too: The plump almond-studded figs, arranged on a bed of bay leaves, glisten with a coating of honey, vinegar, and herb sauce. Over the top goes a generous sprinkling of pungent finely cracked pepper. Serve with Yogurt Cheese (page 18), radishes, and olives.

Makes 8 meze servings

8 bay leaves

8 large, plump dried figs such as Calimyrnas or Atticas, stems trimmed, halved lengthwise

8 blanched almonds, halved lengthwise

1 tablespoon Hymettus or other strongly flavored honey

2 tablespoons red wine vinegar, or 1 tablespoon balsamic vinegar

1 teaspoon dried thyme or marjoram, crumbled

¼ teaspoon finely cracked pepper

Spread the bay leaves over a small platter and arrange the figs on top, cut-sides up. Gently push an almond half into the center of each one.

Combine the honey and vinegar and sprinkle over the figs. Dust with thyme or marjoram and pepper. Serve within 1 hour.

THYME-SCENTED MUSHROOMS

Greece's hot, dry climate means that, for many Greeks, mushrooms are a rare treat. Only those living in the northern countryside or in the hills and mountains can find wild mushrooms, and it's customary to preserve some to give to relatives and friends living in Athens and the south. The mushrooms are usually dried, but in this recipe from Epirus they are preserved in thyme- or Greek oregano-scented vinegar. Delicious with aged kephalotyri cheese and Meze Breads (page 30), or as a pleasing accompaniment to grilled foods or sausages.

Makes 8 meze, or 4 first-course or side-dish servings

4 tablespoons extra-virgin olive oil

¼ teaspoon coarsely ground pepper

4 bay leaves

1 tablespoon red wine vinegar

12 ounces button mushrooms, stems trimmed to ¼ inch, halved or quartered if large

3 sprigs thyme

1 tablespoon water (optional)

Coarse sea salt to taste

In a small, heavy saucepan, combine 2 tablespoons of the olive oil, the pepper, bay leaves, and ½ tablespoon of the vinegar. Warm over very low heat. Add the mushrooms and 2 of the thyme sprigs. Cover the pan with a tight-fitting lid and, holding the lid in place, gently shake the pan. Cook the mushrooms in their own juices for 10 minutes, or until just changing color and still a little firm; stir once or twice with a wooden spoon and add the water if the pan appears dry. Transfer everything to a bowl. Pour over the remaining 2 tablespoons olive oil and ½ tablespoon vinegar. Cover and set aside for at least 1 hour or up to 3 hours.

Discard the thyme sprigs. Transfer the mushrooms mixture to a shallow bowl or platter. Sprinkle with salt and the leaves from the remaining thyme sprig.

STUFFED LEAVES & FLOWERS

Each region has a version of stuffed grape leaves (dolmades), but what makes these so appealing is their sheer daintiness. Small grape leaves, stuffed with a sweet, nutty, mint-perfumed filling, are fashioned into tiny parcels (dolmadakia) for special occasions. The recipe comes from Macedonia, a region home to many Greeks whose families originated from what is now Turkey; the spicy fragrance owes much to that Ottoman influence. Serve with black olives and Yogurt Cheese (page 18), or with grilled meats or game.

This filling can also be used to stuff zucchini flowers. Serve with lemon wedges and a garnish of fresh blossoms, alongside a platter of stuffed grape leaves.

Makes 24 dolmadakia

8 tablespoons extra-virgin olive oil

⅔ cup short-grain rice

1⅓ cups water

Sea salt to taste

2 shallots, minced

¼ cup dried currants

3 tablespoons pine nuts, coarsely chopped and lightly toasted (see page 124)

½ teaspoon ground allspice

6 small fresh mint leaves, minced, or ½ tablespoon dried mint, crumbled

2 tablespoons minced fresh flat-leaf parsley

Freshly ground pepper to taste

Juice of 1 large lemon

About 10 fresh or preserved grape leaves, any size, to line the saucepan, plus 24 small fresh or preserved grape leaves (3 to 4 inches across at the widest point), stems trimmed to ⅛ inch

Lemon wedges for garnish

In a heavy, medium saucepan over low heat, heat 1 tablespoon of the olive oil and add the rice. Cook for 1 minute, stirring occasionally. Add the water and salt. Increase the heat to medium-low, bring to a boil, and cook until the water has disappeared and holes appear on the surface of the rice. Remove from heat, cover the pan with 2 layers of paper towels and a lid, and set aside for 30 minutes.

In a heavy skillet over low heat, heat 3 tablespoons of the olive oil and sauté the shallots for about 5 minutes, or until soft. Add the currants, pine nuts, and allspice and continue cooking for 1 minute; stir in the rice. Stir the mint into the rice with the parsley, salt and pepper to taste, and half the lemon juice. Taste and adjust the seasoning; the filling should be highly flavored.

In a large saucepan of slowly boiling water, blanch 4 or 5 of the grape leaves, 3 seconds for preserved leaves, 5 seconds for fresh. Using a slotted spoon, transfer to paper towels to dry. Repeat to blanch the remaining leaves.

Choose a heavy saucepan, just large enough to comfortably hold the dolmadakia in a single, tightly packed layer. Line the pan with grape leaves, glossy-side down. Lay 1 grape leaf on your palm, glossy-side down and stem towards you, and arrange 1 tablespoon of the filling in the center, ¼ inch in from the stem. Lift the stem over the filling, steady it with your thumb, then fold in the two sides; firmly roll up from the stem end to the point of the leaf to make a package. Place in the saucepan, seam-side down, and repeat with the remaining grape leaves, laying each one firmly against the next. Pour over 2 tablespoons of the olive oil and the remaining lemon juice. Add water to barely reach the top of the dolmadakia. Place a plate, then a weight (such as a can of fruit), on top of the dolmadakia. Gently bring to a low boil, reduce heat, and simmer for 30 minutes. Remove from heat and let cool for at least 15 minutes, leaving the plate and weight in place (this prevents the dolmadakia from unraveling later).

Arrange the dolmadakia on a serving platter and sprinkle with the remaining 2 tablespoons olive oil and the pan juices to taste. Season with salt and pepper to taste. Gently push the lemon wedges, peel-side up, among the dolmadakia.

VARIATION: In place of the 24 grape leaves, use 8 male zucchini blossoms, stems trimmed to ¼ inch (male blossoms, attached to stems instead of the incipient fruit, don't split at the base when stuffed), and 16 fresh grape leaves. To stuff zucchini blossoms, hold one in the palm of your hand and, with your thumb, gently push 1 tablespoon of the filling inside, taking care not to break the blossom. Fold 1 petal over the filling, then fold in the other petals to make a secure package; repeat with the remaining blossoms and filling. Place in the saucepan alongside the stuffed grape leaves.

MEZE BREADS

If throwing away day-old bread goes against your thrifty instincts, try turning it into these crunchy meze snacks. Serve them with soft, strongly flavored foods such as preserved fish appetizers (see page 12), and they are always very popular. Try these meze breads mixed with tomatoes, olives, and watercress, or with radishes, olives, and cucumber chunks, and a glass of ouzo, tsipouro, or wine.

The anchovy version goes well with bean dishes, olives, and green salads, while the cheese version pairs with meat. Serve warm or at room temperature.

Each recipe makes 8 meze servings

SESAME BREAD

Three ¾-inch-thick slices day-old whole-wheat or country-style bread, crusts removed

6 tablespoons extra-virgin olive oil

1 teaspoon coarse sea salt

2 tablespoons sesame seeds

Preheat the oven to 325°F. Cut the bread into 1½-inch-square pieces. Arrange the pieces an inch apart on a baking sheet. Brush the bread with half of the olive oil, and sprinkle with half of the salt and half of the sesame seeds. Bake for 8 to 10 minutes, or until the sesame seeds begin to turn pale gold. Turn the pieces, brush with the remaining olive oil, and sprinkle with the remaining salt and sesame seeds. Bake 6 minutes longer, or until golden.

ANCHOVY BREAD

Three ¾-inch-thick slices day-old
  whole-wheat or country-style
  bread, crusts removed

3 salt-packed anchovy fillets,
  rinsed, soaked, and patted dry
  (see page 118)

½ tablespoon fresh lemon juice

6 tablespoons extra-virgin olive oil

1 tablespoon dried marjoram,
  crumbled

½ tablespoon dried rosemary,
  crushed

Preheat the oven to 325°F. Cut the bread into 1- to 1½-inch-square pieces. Arrange the pieces an inch apart on a baking sheet. Put the anchovy fillets in a mortar or small bowl and mash with a pounder or wooden spoon while adding the lemon juice, drop by drop. Whisk in the olive oil. Brush two-thirds of this sauce over the bread pieces, and sprinkle with half the marjoram and rosemary. Bake for 8 minutes, or until lightly browned; turn the pieces, brush with the remaining sauce, and sprinkle with the remaining marjoram and rosemary. Bake 6 minutes longer, or until browned.

CHEESE BREAD

Three ¾-inch-thick slices day-old
  whole-wheat or country-style
  bread, crusts removed

A few drops of red wine vinegar

6 tablespoons extra-virgin olive oil

¼ cup finely grated kasseri, aged
  kephalotyri, or Italian pecorino
  cheese

1 tablespoon dried Greek oregano or
  rigani, crumbled

Preheat the oven to 325°F. Cut the bread into 1- to 1½-inch-square pieces. Arrange the pieces 1 inch apart on a baking sheet. Combine the vinegar and olive oil, and brush the bread pieces with two-thirds of this sauce. Sprinkle with half the cheese and oregano, and bake for 8 minutes, or until lightly browned. Turn the pieces, brush with the remaining sauce, sprinkle with the rest of the cheese and oregano, and bake for another 6 minutes, or until browned.

SESAME BREAD, page 30

HONEYED WALNUTS

For a few days in early fall, new-crop walnuts drizzled with honey are a delightful meze treat. For sweet snacks later in the season, villagers make these traditional orange-scented walnut candies, popular sweetmeats since the days of antiquity. Dark golden, with a rich flavor and gooey texture, they are served as a sweet meze nibble with coffee and other sweet treats.

For a delightfully simple dessert, lightly crush the candies and sprinkle over ice cream, creamy yogurt, or slices of Manouri cheese. Pistachio nuts or almonds can be candied the same way.

Makes 20 to 24 candies

1 cup Hymettus or other strongly flavored honey

1 teaspoon fresh lemon juice

A few drops vanilla extract

1 cup walnuts or unsalted pistachios, skinned and broken into large pieces (see page 124), or slivered almonds, toasted

½ tablespoon unsalted butter, melted

½ tablespoon orange-flower water

Pour the honey into a heavy saucepan, place over low heat, and slowly bring to a boil, stirring constantly with a wooden spoon; do not burn. Reduce heat still further and simmer for 1 minute. Stir in the lemon juice, vanilla, and nuts. Continue simmering and stirring for about 4 minutes, or until the honey is a deep gold and the nuts begin to sizzle. Remove from heat and stir for 1 minute to prevent further cooking. Stir in the butter.

Divide the mixture among 8 pretty, little dishes or plates and sprinkle with the orange-flower water. Set aside to cool completely.

QUINCE CANDIES

Rich in scented quince flavor and a glorious amber-red in color, these candies were popular sweetmeats in the days of Plato. Modern Greeks, too, have a passion for them, in all their regional variety. Try them flavored with almonds or walnuts or dusted with cinnamon sugar, or store between geranium or bay leaves to give them an exquisite light perfume. Serve quince candies with little cups of Greek coffee and small glasses of Samos Nectar as a sweet meze, or with a barrel-aged feta cheese or fresh white goat cheese for an unusual but traditional meze.

Makes 25 to 30 candies

2 pounds hard, slightly underripe quinces, just turning yellow, fuzzy down wiped off with a kitchen towel

2 lemon quarters, plus 1 tablespoon fresh lemon juice

1 cup water

2 to 3 cups granulated sugar, as needed

25 to 30 walnut pieces or slivered almonds (optional)

⅓ cup superfine sugar

1 scant teaspoon ground cinnamon, or enough lemon- or rose-scented geranium leaves or bay leaves to line container

Peeling quinces is easier if you first soften their skins: Leave them in a large saucepan of slowly boiling water for 1 minute. Fill a large bowl half full with ice water. Squeeze in the juice of the 2 lemon quarters and add the peels. With a small stainless-steel knife (other metals will discolor quince and spoil its flavor), and working quickly, peel, quarter, and core the quinces, then thinly slice or julienne the quince quarters into the ice water. Tie the peels and cores in a square of cheesecloth.

Drain the quince slices and transfer to a large, heavy saucepan. Add the 1 cup water and push the cheesecloth bag down among the slices. Bring to a boil over medium-low heat. Reduce heat to low and simmer for 20 minutes, or until soft, stirring occasionally with a wooden spoon to prevent the fruit from sticking or burning. Remove the cheesecloth bag and leave it to cool in a bowl.

Set a stainless-steel fine-mesh sieve over a bowl and push the quince pulp through with the back of a large spoon. Hold the cheesecloth bag over the bowl and squeeze it to extract as much juice as possible; discard the bag. Measure the pulp, return it to the saucepan, and add an equal amount of granulated sugar. Add the 1 tablespoon lemon juice and slowly simmer until the sugar is dissolved, stirring occasionally with a wooden spoon. Increase the heat to medium-low and boil until the mixture is pastelike and, when stirred, holds its shape and leaves the sides of the saucepan (it will have reduced in volume by between one-quarter and one-third). Don't let it burn; stir frequently with the wooden spoon, and for protection, wrap your hand in a kitchen towel. (If the mixture spits violently, reduce the heat still further.)

Line a jellyroll pan or shallow baking dish with waxed paper and spoon in the quince paste. With a spatula, spread to an even ¾-inch-thick layer and tidy the ends. Let cool. Using a thin-bladed knife, score the paste into 1-inch squares or diamonds; if desired, gently press 1 walnut piece or almond sliver into each candy. Cover the pan with a tea towel and set aside for 2 days to dry (if outside, bring in at night).

Cut through the score marks with the thin-bladed knife to separate the candies. Line an airtight container with waxed paper. Combine the superfine sugar and cinnamon and roll each candy in this mixture. Layer the candies in the container between sheets of waxed paper. Or, line the container with geranium or bay leaves and layer the candies on top; separate each layer with leaves or waxed paper. Store in a cool spot for up to 3 months.

COLD PLATES

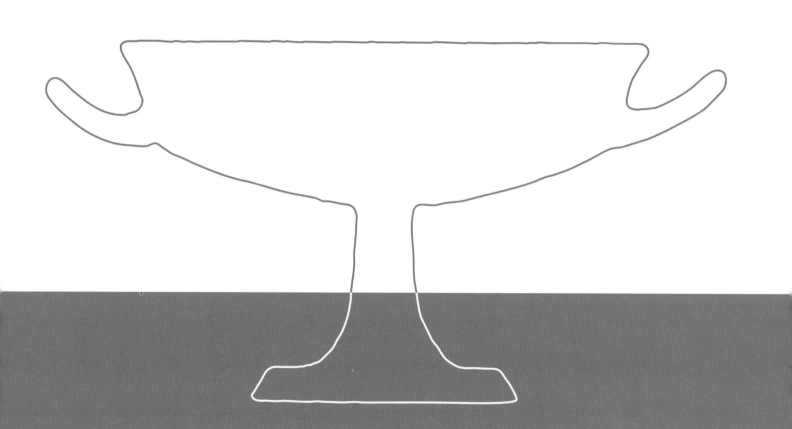

The cold meze table has few rivals in any cuisine. It includes meat, chicken, or game steeped in piquant marinades; just-caught fish, shellfish, octopus, and squid; fresh cheeses and sun-ripened fruit; and a riot of vegetables cloaked in light sauces. Above all, the emphasis is on freshness and abundance.

Many of the dishes have historical interest and echo the diverse influences on Greek cuisine over the centuries. There are spicy eggplant dishes made popular by Greeks returning from Smyrna, fruit-and-nut combinations of Jewish festival cooking, and vivacious Balkan dishes that were favorites of the long-ago merchants and diplomats of the Ottoman Empire.

These are perfect picnic and party foods. Most of the dishes in this chapter can be prepared well ahead of time and need little last-minute attention. Two or three, along with plenty of crusty bread, make a splendid outdoor spread, and quantities can easily be doubled or tripled for a large gathering. Served alone, they make imaginative, healthy light lunches or suppers.

What strikes a newcomer to the delights of the cold meze table is the sheer variety of the dishes and the novelty of discovery, the pleasure of eating the freshest food in its proper season, and the exuberance or subtlety of color and taste.

SMALL FISH IN A SWEET & SAVORY SAUCE

This piquant dish has both historic and gastronomic interest. After cooking, the fish rests in a marinating sauce composed of some favorite flavors of ancient Greece: sweet wine, honey, currants, vinegar, coriander, and bay leaves. Although the dish has changed little since the days of antiquity, the pepper strips in this recipe are a Byzantine addition.

The marinade deepens and sharpens the flavor of the fish, while enhancing it with spicy scent. The finished dish is mellow and succulent, with a gorgeous rich color. Sea bass, fresh tuna, or swordfish may be substituted.

Makes 8 meze or first-course servings

8 red mullet or other small fish, 3 to 4 ounces each, heads intact, or 1 pound fish fillets, cut into 8 serving pieces

Sea salt and freshly ground pepper to taste

8 tablespoons extra-virgin olive oil

4 slender yellow Anaheim chilies, about 3 inches long, or 2 small red bell peppers, roasted, peeled, and cut into thin lengthwise strips (see page 123)

1 tablespoon red wine vinegar

½ teaspoon ground coriander

⅓ cup dried currants or small seedless raisins, soaked for 30 minutes in 2 tablespoons hot water

4 bay leaves

1 teaspoon honey

¼ cup Malmsey or Madeira wine, or 2 tablespoons hot water

16 Elitses or niçoise olives

3 tablespoons coarsely chopped fresh flat-leaf parsley or cilantro

If using whole fish, rinse and pat dry. Rub the fish inside and out (or fillets on both sides) with salt and pepper. Arrange on a plate in a single layer. Cover with plastic wrap and set aside for 30 minutes.

In a large, heavy skillet over low heat, heat 3 tablespoons of the olive oil. Sauté the fish on both sides, turning once with a spatula, for about 8 minutes, or until opaque throughout. Drain on paper towels and transfer to a bowl or arrange on a serving platter.

Pour out the oil and wipe the skillet with paper towels. Return the pan to low heat and warm 3 tablespoons of the olive oil. Add the chilies or peppers and gently stir to coat. Cook for a minute or two, sprinkle with the vinegar, and continue cooking for 1 minute. Add the coriander, currants or raisins, and any remaining water, the bay leaves, and honey. Simmer for 2 minutes, stirring once or twice. Add the wine or water and simmer 2 minutes longer. Pour this sauce over the fish and set aside to cool.

To serve now, sprinkle with olives and parsley. Pour over the remaining 2 tablespoons olive oil. To store for up to 24 hours, put the fish and sauce in a bowl and pour over the remaining 2 tablespoons olive oil. Cover and refrigerate; turn the fish once or twice in the marinade. For serving, bring back to room temperature and sprinkle with olives and parsley.

FISH UNDER A BLANKET

This is the perfect recipe for adding zest to fish that's low on flavor. Fillets of white fish coated with sauce are served with black-eyed peas, sweet red onion, and fresh herbs.

Makes 8 meze or 4 first-course servings

¾ cup dried black-eyed peas

1 pound raw or cooked fish fillets or pieces

2 oil-packed sun-dried tomatoes, drained and diced

1 tablespoon salt-packed capers, soaked, rinsed, and patted dry (see page 118)

6 Thasos or other black salt-cured olives, pitted and chopped

Freshly ground pepper to taste

7 tablespoons extra-virgin olive oil

1 teaspoon preserved lemon (see page 124), or ½ teaspoon grated organic lemon zest

½ tablespoon fresh lemon juice

½ teaspoon coarse sea salt

½ small red onion, finely chopped, or 2 green onions, including green parts, finely chopped

3 tablespoons coarsely chopped fresh flat-leaf parsley

3 tablespoons coarsely chopped fresh cilantro, chervil, watercress, arugula, borage, mint, thyme, marjoram, or basil, or a mixture

½ cup Village Yogurt (page 17)

Rinse and pick over the peas. Soak in water to cover by 2 inches overnight; drain. Put the peas in a large saucepan with cold water to cover. Bring to a boil, simmer for 5 minutes, then drain; rinse both peas and pan. Return the peas to the saucepan and add cold water to cover by at least 3 inches. Bring to a boil, reduce heat, cover, and simmer for 20 minutes, or until tender.

Check to make sure the fish is completely free of bones and divide it into 8 portions. To cook raw fish, either steam or bake it: To steam the fish, cook in a covered steamer over simmering water for 15 minutes, or until opaque throughout. To bake the fish, pour ¼ cup of water into a heavy baking dish and heat in a preheated 375°F oven. Arrange the fish pieces in the dish, cover with aluminum foil, and bake for 20 minutes, or until opaque. Using a metal spatula, transfer the fish to paper towels to drain. Arrange on one side of a platter or on individual plates. Set aside.

In a food processor, combine the tomatoes, ½ tablespoon of the capers, the olives, and pepper. Process to mix. With the machine running, gradually add 5 tablespoons of the olive oil. Spread the sauce neatly over each piece of fish.

On a cutting board, chop together the preserved lemon or lemon zest, salt, and remaining ½ tablespoon capers. Transfer to a medium bowl and stir in the lemon juice and remaining 2 tablespoons olive oil. Add the black-eyed peas, onion or green onions, parsley, cilantro or other herbs, and pepper to taste. Stir to mix. Arrange this mixture alongside the fish on the platter or on the individual plates. Heap the yogurt alongside or on top of the beans and serve.

SFAKIA OCTOPUS

Tsipouro *is Crete's national firewater (see page 127). At its best, it has a fine, subtle flavor all too easily overwhelmed by assertive food flavors. So, when villagers in the island's Sfakia province come by some good tsipouro, this is the meze they serve with it: an understated dish of octopus marinated for 2 days in vinegar, garlic, and dried Greek oregano or rigani. Complement with A Warm Salad of Bitter Greens (page 64) and plenty of Meze Breads (page 30) to mop up the delicious sauce.*

Makes 8 to 10 meze or 6 first-course servings

One 2-pound octopus or octopus piece, tenderized and cleaned

1½ cups red wine vinegar

3 to 6 cloves garlic (to taste)

2 large sprigs dried Greek oregano or rigani, plus 1 tablespoon dried Greek oregano or rigani, crumbled

⅓ cup extra-virgin olive oil

2 tablespoons minced fresh flat-leaf parsley

1 teaspoon coarsely ground pepper

1 tablespoon salt-packed small capers, soaked, rinsed, and patted dry (see page 118)

16 Elitses or niçoise olives

Coarse sea salt to taste (optional)

In a large nonreactive saucepan, combine the octopus and ½ cup of the vinegar. Add water to cover and bring to a boil over low heat. Cover and reduce heat to very low. Simmer for about 45 minutes, or until the octopus turns deep pink and you can easily push off a tentacle disc (sucker) with a wooden spoon (avoid using metal). Don't overcook, or the octopus will become rubbery later, in the marinade. Drain, peel off the skin, and put the octopus in a bowl. Let cool, then cover and refrigerate for 1 or 2 hours to chill.

Cut the octopus into 1½- to 2-inch pieces. Rinse out the bowl and return the octopus to the bowl. Press down on each garlic clove with the side of a heavy knife until the clove splits and add them to the bowl with the oregano sprigs and the remaining 1 cup vinegar. Cover the bowl and refrigerate for 2 days, stirring occasionally with a wooden spoon.

To serve, drain the octopus in a nonreactive colander. Discard the garlic and oregano sprigs. Transfer to a platter, pour over the olive oil, and sprinkle with the 1 tablespoon oregano, the parsley, pepper, capers, olives, and a little salt, if desired.

YOGURT CHICKEN WITH BEETS & GREENS

This is the dish to put center stage on your summer meze table—it has immediate visual appeal and satisfying contrasts of texture. The creamy herb-poached chicken sits alongside a glossy salad of purple-red beets tossed with greens.

Surround this irresistible star of the show with dishes of black olives, seasonal vegetable mezes, and golden Meze Breads (page 30). For everyday meals, simply serve with olives and crusty bread.

Makes 8 meze or first-course servings, or 4 light main-course servings

1 small chicken (about 2¼ pounds), cut into serving pieces, or 1¼ pounds chicken serving pieces

3 cups light chicken broth, water, or a mixture

6 sprigs basil

6 sprigs parsley

6 small beets with greens (about 1 pound), greens reserved, baked (see page 60)

¼ teaspoon ground allspice

Coarse sea salt and freshly ground pepper to taste

½ cup Village Yogurt (page 17)

½ teaspoon Dijon mustard

½ teaspoon honey

1 teaspoon red wine vinegar or a few drops of balsamic vinegar

3 tablespoons extra-virgin olive oil

In a large, heavy saucepan, combine the chicken, broth and/or water, basil, and parsley. Cover and bring to a boil over medium-low heat. Reduce heat to low and simmer for about 35 minutes, or until tender. Place a colander or sieve over a bowl and drain the chicken; set the chicken and broth aside to cool.

Peel and trim the beets. Cut the beets into ¼-inch-thick half-moons or large matchsticks and put in a medium bowl. Sprinkle with the allspice and set aside.

Strip the beet leaves from the stalks. In a large, nonreactive saucepan, bring ½ cup of water to a boil, add the greens, cover, and cook for 1 minute. Drain in a colander, pressing with the back of a large spoon to squeeze out liquid. Transfer to a cutting board and coarsely chop the greens.

Spoon off the fat from the chicken broth. Measure out ½ cup broth and strain it into a small saucepan (freeze the remainder for future use). Bring to a boil over medium-high heat and continue boiling until reduced to 3 tablespoons. Pour into a bowl and set aside until cold.

Discard the chicken skin and bones and cut the chicken into bite-sized pieces. Season the broth with salt and pepper. Whisk in the yogurt. Add the chicken and, with a spoon, turn in the sauce to coat each piece. Taste and adjust the seasoning. Arrange the chicken and sauce on one side of a platter.

Add the greens to the beets and gently mix everything together; take care not to break the beets. In a small bowl, whisk together the mustard, honey, vinegar, and olive oil. Pour over the beet mixture. Sprinkle with salt and pepper, gently toss to mix, and arrange on the platter alongside the chicken. Serve immediately.

SALT-BAKED EGGPLANT & RED PEPPER SALATA

Pungent eggplant salates (salads) are popular throughout the Near and Middle East. This Greek version has a coarse but creamy texture and a chorus of tongue-tingling tastes: earthy eggplant, hot green onion, musky sesame seed, fresh parsley, and sweet red pepper. All these notes are blended to a piquant counterpoint with red wine vinegar, muted on serving with a little thick, creamy yogurt.

The layer of salt under the baking eggplants is essential to give them a special flavor and a soft but firm texture, and it also draws out and absorbs the vegetable's bitter juices. Serve with Meze Breads (page 30) and olives.

Makes 8 meze or 4 first-course servings

3 eggplants (6 to 7 ounces each), stemmed and rinsed

¼ cup plus ½ teaspoon coarse sea salt

1 tablespoon stirred tahini (sesame paste)

1 tablespoon red wine vinegar

¼ cup extra-virgin olive oil

¼ cup chopped fresh flat-leaf parsley

¼ teaspoon freshly ground pepper

1 red bell pepper, roasted, peeled, and cut into thin strips (see page 123)

2 green onions, including unblemished green parts, trimmed and cut into diagonal slivers

4 tablespoons Village Yogurt (page 17)

½ teaspoon sumac

Preheat the oven to 375°F. With a small, sharp knife, make a shallow lengthwise incision around the center of each eggplant and prick all over. Spread the ¼ cup salt in a heavy, shallow baking dish and place the eggplants on top. Bake uncovered, for 40 to 50 minutes, or until the skins are shriveled and browned.

Remove from the oven and let cool to the touch. Split each eggplant open at the center incision. With a spoon, scoop the flesh out onto a chopping board; discard the skins. Chop the flesh into small dice and put in a large bowl.

In a small bowl, mix the tahini and vinegar together, then whisk in the olive oil. Pour this sauce over the eggplant and gently stir to mix. Put the parsley, pepper, and the ½ teaspoon salt on a cutting board and chop them together. Sprinkle this mixture over the eggplant. Add the bell pepper, green onions, and 3 tablespoons of the yogurt. Very gently mix everything together. Taste and adjust the seasoning. Transfer to a shallow serving bowl or platter. Garnish with the remaining 1 tablespoon yogurt and sprinkle with the sumac. Serve immediately.

FRESH FIGS WITH YOGURT CHEESE

I love the country simplicity of this meze—my favorite when sweet ripe figs are available. It's a dish of contrasts: the green and white of the thyme-speckled yogurt cheese and the deep purple of the figs, the sweetness of the figs and the tang of yogurt, and crunch of the walnuts with the smooth, creamy yogurt and succulent fruit. This is excellent with pastourmas or prosciutto, Parma ham, or with a green salad, Aromatic Olives (page 15), and Meze Breads (page 30).

Makes 8 meze servings

Yogurt Cheese (page 18) or one 8-ounce log fresh white goat cheese

8 Black Mission or other figs, halved lengthwise

½ cup walnut halves

½ teaspoon coarsely ground pepper, or to taste

2 tablespoons extra-virgin olive oil, or to taste

1 tablespoon minced fresh thyme, or ½ tablespoon dried thyme, crumbled

Mound the yogurt cheese in the center of a platter, or cut the goat cheese into 8 slices and place on the platter. Surround with the figs, cut-side up. Heap the walnuts to one side of the platter. Sprinkle both the figs and cheese with pepper. Sprinkle the cheese with olive oil and thyme. Serve immediately.

TINY ARTICHOKES WITH LEMON MAYONNAISE

This dish is a classic example of letting good ingredients speak for themselves: lightly boiled or steamed artichokes, marinated in olive oil seasoned with lemon juice, Greek oregano, and bay leaves. They're served with a lemon mayonnaise lightly flavored with anchovy, capers, and parsley. The mayonnaise should be made no more than an hour or two before serving.

Choose small violet-leafed artichokes or baby artichokes for this dish and, if possible, make the mayonnaise with Greek extra-virgin olive oil. The mayonnaise is also good with cold fish and meats, or with cold cooked beets or potatoes. Serve with green onions and olives.

Makes 8 meze or 4 first-course servings

1 tablespoon flour

1 teaspoon fine sea salt, plus more to taste

Juice of 2 small lemons, shells reserved

16 baby artichokes, or 8 small artichokes

½ teaspoon Dijon mustard

Coarsely ground pepper to taste

1 tablespoon dried Greek oregano or rigani, crumbled

½ cup extra-virgin olive oil

3 bay leaves

1 salt-packed anchovy fillet, rinsed, soaked, and patted dry (see page 118)

(continued on page 48)

1 tablespoon salt-packed capers,
  soaked, rinsed, and patted dry
  (see page 118)

Leaves from 12 sprigs flat-leaf
  parsley, minced

1 large organic egg yolk

Fill a large nonreactive saucepan half full of water and bring to a boil. Fill a large bowl with ice water. Whisk in the flour and the 1 teaspoon salt. Add 2 of the reserved lemon half-shells (the flour, salt, and citric acid help prevent the artichokes from discoloring). Remove the outer leaves of one of the artichokes, leaving only the tender light-green ones. Leave baby artichokes intact, but remove the chokes from small artichokes: With a sharp knife, slice off the top third of the artichoke and scoop out the fuzzy choke with a small spoon. Rub the cut surface with a lemon half-shell and add the artichoke to the bowl of ice water. Repeat with the remaining artichokes.

Drain the artichokes and add to the boiling water (discard the half-shells). Reduce the heat to a brisk simmer, cover, and cook the baby artichokes for 20 minutes or the small artichokes for 30 minutes, or until just tender. Drain and spread on paper towels to dry.

In a medium bowl, whisk the mustard, 1 tablespoon of the lemon juice, salt to taste, pepper, oregano, and 3 tablespoons of the olive oil together. Add the bay leaves and artichokes and stir to coat with the marinade. Cover and refrigerate for at least 1 hour or up to 3 hours.

In a food processor or mortar, combine the anchovy, capers, and parsley, and pulse or pound until well mixed. Add the egg yolk and pulse or pound to blend. With the machine running, or with a whisk, gradually blend in the remaining 5 tablespoons olive oil in a thin, steady stream. Gradually add 1 tablespoon lemon juice.

Arrange the artichokes on a serving platter and pour the marinade over. Serve the lemon mayonnaise alongside. Serve immediately.

e/oe/oe/oe/oe/oe/o

VARIATION: If you need to make the mayonnaise more than an hour or two ahead, omit the anchovy. Left in a sauce, its flavor tends to dominate.

e/oe/oe/oe/oe/oe/o

SANTORINI SPLIT PEAS

This pale-yellow vegetable dish from the island of Santorini has visual appeal; a gentle, spicy taste and a soft earthy texture. The islanders make it with a sweet yellow split-pea variety I have yet to find outside the Cyclades, so to produce the "Santorini effect," this recipe adds the sweetener of carrot and onion. Serve with Meze Breads (page 30) and Tiny Tomatoes with Green Olive Sauce (page 56).

Makes 8 meze or 4 first-course servings

1 cup yellow split peas, rinsed

1 large carrot, peeled and cut into large pieces

2 bay leaves

1 small onion, stuck with 2 cloves

1 small ½-inch-thick slice coarse-textured white or whole-wheat bread, crust removed, lightly toasted

2 tablespoons milk

4 to 6 tablespoons extra-virgin olive oil

¼ teaspoon ground cumin

1 teaspoon fine sea salt

¼ teaspoon freshly ground pepper

½ tablespoon red wine vinegar

1 tablespoon salt-packed small capers, soaked, rinsed, and patted dry (see page 118)

1 tablespoon finely chopped green onion leaves

2 tablespoons chopped fresh dill, fennel fronds, or flat-leaf parsley

Soak the peas in cold water for 4 to 6 hours, changing the water twice during that time. Drain the peas, put them in a large saucepan, and add water to cover. Bring to a boil over medium-low heat. Drain and rinse both peas and pan. Return the peas to the saucepan. Add the carrot, bay leaves, onion, and water to cover by 2 inches. Bring to a boil over medium-low heat. Reduce heat to a simmer, cover, and cook for 30 to 40 minutes, or until the peas are soft. Drain in a colander set over a bowl; measure and set aside ½ cup of the cooking liquid. Discard the carrot, bay leaves, and onion.

Tear the toast into small pieces. Put them in a small bowl, add the milk, and soak for 5 minutes. Transfer the peas to a food processor. Using the pulse switch, gradually add 3 tablespoons of the olive oil. Add the bread pieces, cumin, salt, pepper, and vinegar, and pulse to mix. Still using the pulse switch, gradually add the reserved cooking liquid and 1 to 3 tablespoons olive oil as needed to make a stiff mixture; stop pulsing before smooth. Taste and adjust the seasoning.

Spread over a platter and sprinkle with the capers, green onion, and herb.

OKRA IN RICH TOMATO SAUCE

The sweet tomato sauce, lively with coriander and cinnamon, keeps the okra in this dish juicy and flavorful. The flavors will even improve if you make it a day ahead. This is a wonderfully practical dish to serve as the centerpiece of a meat-free meze table, with olives, cheese, a green salad, and Meze Breads (page 30).

Use the same sauce with other fresh vegetables or cooked beans to accompany grilled chicken or fish, or sfongata (page 86).

Makes 8 meze or 4 side-dish servings

1 pound okra

4 cups water

¼ cup red wine vinegar

RICH TOMATO SAUCE

3 tablespoons extra-virgin olive oil

1½ onions, quartered and thinly sliced

1 plump clove garlic, minced (optional)

1 teaspoon ground coriander

½ teaspoon ground cinnamon

12 ounces tomatoes, peeled and diced (juices reserved)

1 teaspoon Hymettus or other strongly flavored honey

½ tablespoon tomato paste diluted in 2 tablespoons water

Coarse sea salt and coarsely ground pepper to taste

½ cup coarsely chopped fresh flat-leaf parsley

5 tablespoons extra-virgin olive oil

½ tablespoon red wine vinegar

Trim off the tips and stems of the okra (avoid cutting into the pod or it will burst later). Pour the water into a large bowl and stir in the vinegar with a wooden spoon. Add the okra and soak for 30 minutes. Drain, rinse under cold running water, and spread on paper towels to dry (this process helps the okra to stay intact during cooking).

Meanwhile, make the tomato sauce: In a medium, heavy nonreactive saucepan over low heat, heat the 3 tablespoons of olive oil and sauté the onions, stirring occasionally, for about 20 minutes, or until pale golden; don't let them brown. Add the garlic, if using, and cook until fragrant, 2 or 3 minutes. Stir in the coriander and cinnamon, cook for 1 minute, then add the tomatoes and their juices, the honey, tomato paste mixture, salt, and pepper. Increase the heat to medium-low and continue cooking until the sauce thickens enough to leave a path for a few seconds when a wooden spoon is drawn across the bottom of the pan. Stir in half the parsley and remove the pan from heat.

In a large, heavy skillet over low heat, heat 3 tablespoons of the olive oil and sauté the okra for about 4 minutes or until faintly darkened. Using a wooden spoon, transfer to paper towels to drain. Carefully transfer the okra to the tomato sauce. Lightly cover the saucepan and simmer for 30 minutes, or until the okra is just tender; add a few tablespoons of water if the sauce appears a little dry. Taste and adjust the seasoning. Holding the lid in place, firmly but gently shake the pan to mix everything together. Transfer the okra and sauce to a shallow serving bowl or platter and set aside to cool.

Sprinkle the okra mixture with the vinegar, the remaining, parsley, and the remaining 2 tablespoons olive oil. Adjust the seasoning. Serve at room temperature.

೧/ᴈ/ᴈ/ᴈ/ᴈ/ᴈ/ᴈ

VARIATION: Many vegetables can be cooked this way. Blanch tiny artichoke hearts, cauliflower florets, or small potatoes before adding to the sauce. Or, sauté slender leeks, tiny whole zucchini, or small onions or shallots in olive oil and add to the sauce; flavor with allspice and dried Greek oregano or rigani instead of cinnamon and parsley. Best of all are young fava beans, tender enough to cook in the pod (see page 120); simmer the beans for 5 minutes before you add them to the sauce, and flavor with fresh fennel fronds instead of parsley.

೧/ᴈ/ᴈ/ᴈ/ᴈ/ᴈ/ᴈ

OLIVE-STUFFED ONIONS

*In the towns and villages at the southern tip of the
Taygetus Mountains in the Peloponnese, the Byzantine
influence is still powerfully present both in the architecture
and the cuisine. This aromatic meze comes from Aeropolis,
a village filled with pomegranate trees that burst into
blood-red blossoms in summer.*

*The delicate appearance of this dish belies its richness of
flavor. The tiniest onions, stuffed with a blend of olives,
walnuts, dried Greek oregano or rigani, and toasted bread
crumbs, are moistened with pomegranate molasses and
gently baked with bay leaves. Serve as part of a mixed platter or on a buffet table.*

Makes 8 meze or 4 first-course servings

¾ cup brown lentils, picked over and
  rinsed

16 boiling onions (about 1 pound),
  1 to 1½ inches in diameter

8 Thasos or other salt-cured
  black olives

5 tablespoons extra-virgin olive oil

¼ cup walnuts, coarsely chopped

2 tablespoons fresh coarse whole-
  wheat bread crumbs, toasted
  (see page 118)

½ tablespoon dried Greek oregano or
  rigani, crumbled

⅓ cup minced fresh flat-leaf parsley

Coarsely ground pepper to taste

4 bay leaves

¼ cup pomegranate molasses,
  diluted with 3 tablespoons water

½ teaspoon Hymettus or other
  strongly flavored honey

Pinch of ground allspice

Coarse sea salt to taste

Put the lentils in a saucepan, add water to cover by 2 inches,
and bring to a boil over medium-low heat. Reduce heat to
low, cover, and simmer for 15 to 20 minutes, or until just
tender. Drain and set aside to cool.

Neatly trim off the onion root ends and remove a ¼-inch
slice from each stem end. In a medium saucepan of boiling
water, cook the onions for 10 minutes. Drain and set aside
to cool.

Preheat the oven to 325°F. Remove the onion skins with a
paring knife. With the knife tip, pull out each onion center
through its stem end, leaving 2 outer layers as a shell.
Using a large knife, chop the onion centers into small dice
and set aside. Stand the shells, root-ends down, in a heavy,
shallow baking dish just large enough to hold the onions
in one layer.

Blanch the olives in boiling water for 5 seconds. Drain, pit, and finely chop.

In a medium, heavy skillet over low heat, heat 1½ tablespoons of the olive oil and cook the chopped onion, stirring occasionally, for about 8 minutes, or until starting to color. Add the olives, walnuts, bread crumbs, oregano, half the parsley, and the pepper; stir to mix. With a small spoon, carefully fill the onion shells with this mixture. Sprinkle with 1½ tablespoons of the remaining olive oil. Add the bay leaves and pomegranate molasses mixture to the dish. Bake, uncovered, for 40 minutes, or until the pan juices are syrupy, basting once or twice.

Whisk together 2 tablespoons of the pan juices, the honey, allspice, and remaining 2 tablespoons olive oil. Stir in more pan juices to taste. Carefully mix this sauce with the lentils and season with salt and pepper to taste. Spread the lentils over a small platter and arrange the onions on top. Sprinkle with the remaining parsley. Serve at room temperature.

SWEET & SOUR SHALLOTS

Long, slow cooking is the secret of this rich, aromatic meze with its origins in ancient recipes for dishes of wild bulbs and leeks. Gently baked with bay leaves, olive oil, wine, red wine vinegar, currants, and honey, the shallots are meltingly soft and mellow and the sauce thick and tangy. Small onions, plump green onions, young leeks, or tiny carrots may be substituted for the shallots.

Serve on a meze table with bean dishes, khorta, olives, slices of aged graviera, aged kephalotyri, or feta cheese, or as a side dish to preserved meats; grilled pork, chicken, or game; or roasted beets.

Makes 8 meze or 4 side-dish servings

24 shallots (about 14 ounces)

2 tablespoons extra-virgin olive oil

4 bay leaves

¼ cup red wine vinegar, or 2 tablespoons balsamic vinegar mixed with 2 tablespoons water

¼ cup dried currants or small seedless dark raisins

2 tablespoons Hymettus or other strongly flavored honey

¼ cup Mavrodaphne, Madeira, or port wine

Coarse sea salt and coarsely ground pepper to taste

Neatly trim off the shallot root ends and remove a very thin slice from each stem end. In a medium saucepan of boiling water, cook the shallots for 5 minutes. Drain and set aside to cool.

Choose a heavy, shallow baking dish just large enough to hold the shallots in a single layer. Place in the oven and preheat the oven to 325°F. Remove the shallot skins with a paring knife. Pour the olive oil into the baking dish. Add the shallots, turn in the oil to coat, and tuck the bay leaves among them. Bake, uncovered, for 20 minutes.

Meanwhile, combine the vinegar, or vinegar and water, and currants or raisins in a small bowl. Stir the honey into the currant or raisin mixture and add this sauce and the wine to the shallots. Baste the shallots and continue baking for 40 minutes to 1 hour, or until the sauce is syrupy. Baste occasionally; if the dish appears dry, add a few tablespoons of water and lightly cover with aluminum foil.

Transfer the shallots to a serving platter or shallow bowl and pour the sauce and bay leaves over. Sprinkle with salt and pepper. Serve at room temperature.

TINY TOMATOES WITH GREEN OLIVE SAUCE

Santorini islanders make this meze with local crimson tomatoes that are tiny, sweet, and packed with flavor from the island's mineral-rich, volcanic-ash soil. The pungent country sauce features green olives, capers, a hint of garlic, and olive oil sharpened with vinegar. The sauce is also good with Siphnos Shrimp Kephtedes (page 78).

Makes 8 meze or 4 first-course servings

2 tablespoons extra-virgin olive oil

24 cherry tomatoes

GREEN OLIVE SAUCE

1 cup cracked green Greek olives or Nafplion olives, or brine-packed Spanish green olives with pits

1½ tablespoons salt-packed capers, soaked, rinsed, and patted dry (see page 118)

1 small clove garlic, minced

1 teaspoon red wine vinegar

3 to 4 tablespoons extra-virgin olive oil

2 tablespoons coarsely chopped fresh fennel fronds or flat-leaf parsley for garnish

2 slices whole-wheat or country-style bread, toasted

In a small, heavy skillet over very low heat, heat the olive oil. Add the tomatoes, cover, and cook for about 3 minutes, or until their skins split. Set aside in the skillet to cool.

To make the sauce: Blanch the olives in boiling water for 5 seconds. Drain, pit, and chop. In a food processor, combine the olives, capers, and garlic. Process until well mixed. With the machine running, add the vinegar, drop by drop, then the olive oil (to taste) in a steady stream.

Spread the sauce over a small platter. Using a slotted spoon, transfer the tomatoes to the platter. Garnish with fennel or parsley. Cut the crusts from the toast and cut each slice into 4 triangles and arrange on the platter. Sprinkle the bread with the liquid remaining in the tomato pan.

ᘒᘒᘒᘒᘒᘒ

VARIATION: Although it takes more work, this dish is at its traditional best when the olives, capers, and garlic are mashed in a mortar or bowl before you add the vinegar and olive oil. The sauce texture will be coarser, but its flavor will be more refined.

ᘒᘒᘒᘒᘒᘒ

MUSTARD ASPARAGUS & NEW POTATOES

For a few short weeks in spring, wild asparagus carpets the rocky ravines along the long, rugged Greek coastline. Its fresh, clean taste is a welcome change after winter foods, and villagers regard it as a valuable blood cleanser.

The sauce is simple, although its combination of mustard, honey, allspice, vinegar, and olive oil may sound heavy-handed for asparagus. But trust me: It works exceedingly well with asparagus and artichoke hearts, young leeks, green beans, or beets. Enjoy this on its own as a meze dish or with grilled liver, meat, or sausages.

Makes 8 meze or 4 first-course or side-dish servings

8 ounces slender asparagus

1 tablespoon Meaux mustard, or ½ tablespoon Dijon mustard

½ tablespoon Hymettus or other strongly flavored honey

Generous pinch of ground allspice

1 tablespoon red wine vinegar, or ½ tablespoon balsamic vinegar

¼ cup extra-virgin olive oil

8 ounces small new potatoes, such as Yukon Gold or Yellow Finn, scrubbed and baked (see page 60)

Coarse sea salt and finely cracked pepper to taste

Break off each asparagus stalk at the lowest point where it easily snaps. In a large sauté pan or skillet of briskly simmering water, cook the asparagus for 3 to 4 minutes, or until crisp-tender. Drain and spread on paper towels to dry.

In a large, shallow bowl, whisk the mustard, honey, allspice, vinegar, and olive oil together. Add the asparagus and carefully turn to coat with the marinade. Cover and set aside for at least 1 hour or up to 3 hours.

Drain the asparagus, reserving the marinade, and heap it on one side of a platter. Cut the potatoes into ¼-inch-thick slices and arrange alongside the asparagus. Taste the reserved marinade and add more vinegar and/or olive oil, if you like. Pour the marinade over the potatoes. Sprinkle both asparagus and potatoes with salt and pepper.

GREENS & SALADS

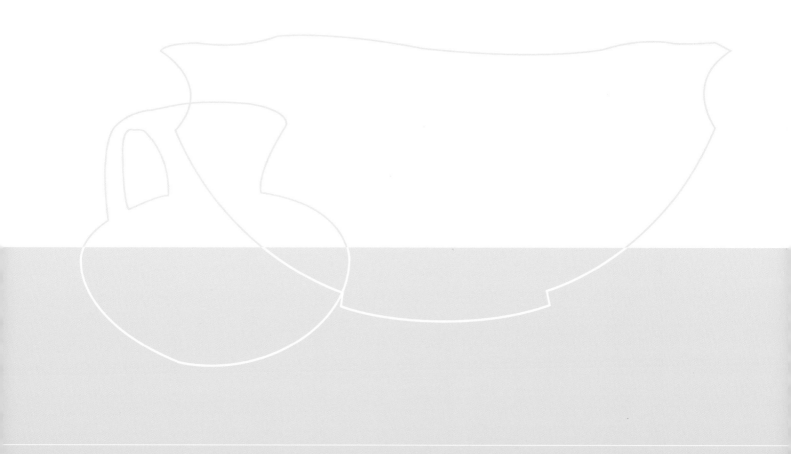

Green salad appears on every Greek table, except in high summer when the weather is too hot for greens to grow. But, with the exception of romaine, the mild, sweet lettuces most of us buy or grow are almost unknown in Greek markets. Instead, the everyday greens are the strongly flavored peppery or bitter greens of the countryside: purslane, watercress, chicory, or young dandelions. Young, tender greens are served just as they are; older greens are usually cooked and served at room temperature or warm.

In our markets, watercress, arugula, beet greens, and turnip greens are relatively easy to find, but you can occasionally also come by dandelion greens and several varieties of chicory. If none of these is available, use spinach, which has the advantage of being easier to prepare than the other greens though it lacks their characteristic sprightly bite.

The earthy, slightly bitter flavor that eastern Mediterraneans love is an acquired taste, but it gives a surprising and welcome jolt to jaded palates and tired taste buds. It's important not to overpower the distinctive bitterness with other flavors; a simple traditional dressing of lemon juice or red wine vinegar with olive oil is the only enhancement needed.

Salads of vegetables and pulses are popular mezes, too: fresh fava beans, zucchini, eggplant, and tomatoes in summer; olives, dried beans or lentils, and preserved vegetables later in the year.

These salads capture the essence of the meze table: the lively taste, the accent on earthy flavors, the aim to stimulate the appetite. For us, the bonus is their excellent nutritional credentials. All are rich in vitamins, minerals, and fiber.

PURSLANE & BEETS

When I first tried purslane, its sharp, peppery bite was a revelation, and this is still one of my favorite salads. It brings together crisp green onions and cucumber, sweet baked beets, olive oil, and spicy purslane to create a satisfying, quick meal with textural contrasts and intense flavor.

It's a great one-dish salad to serve with feta cheese and olives, and it pairs well with grilled meats, too. Try substituting new potatoes, tomatoes, or fava beans for the beets.

Makes 8 meze or 4 side-dish servings

4 small beets, or 6 small new potatoes (about 10 ounces), baked (see instructions) or boil until just tender

1 teaspoon sumac

4 tablespoons extra-virgin olive oil

1 tablespoon fresh lemon juice

Coarse sea salt and freshly ground pepper to taste

3 cups small purslane sprigs

½ English (hothouse) cucumber, peeled and diced

¼ cup coarsely chopped fresh flat-leaf parsley

3 green onions, including unblemished green parts, trimmed and cut into diagonal slivers

One hour before serving, cut the beets or potatoes into halves or quarters and put in a bowl. Sprinkle with the sumac and 1 tablespoon of the olive oil; stir to mix with a wooden spoon.

In a small bowl, whisk together the lemon juice, the remaining 3 tablespoons olive oil, and salt and pepper to taste. Add the purslane, cucumber, and sauce to the beets or potatoes. Gently mix together with a wooden spoon. Transfer to a shallow bowl or platter, sprinkle with the parsley and green onions, and serve immediately.

BAKED BEETS OR POTATOES: Choose small vegetables; scrub, but don't peel. Cut off beet greens ¼ inch from beets. Bake in a covered clay pot in preheated 325°F oven for 1½ to 2 hours, or until tender when pierced with a knife. Let cool to the touch. Peel and slice. Use in a recipe, or toss with a dressing, coarse sea salt, freshly ground pepper, and chopped fresh flat-leaf parsley or an herb of choice and serve as a meze or side dish.

PLAKA SUMMER SALAD

The ancient Plaka district of Athens, nestling beneath the Acropolis, has a cosmopolitan community life which, for fifty years, has been dominated by Marika's Kafenion (café). This meze salad is one of its specialties.

For this simple salad, fresh lettuce and spinach leaves, green onions, and fresh mint are tossed in olive oil, then sprinkled with lemon juice. The finishing touch is a scattering of black olives and feta cheese: delicious, simple, and authentically Greek.

Makes 8 meze or 4 first-course servings

1 handful of fresh young spinach leaves, stemmed

Tender inner leaves from 1 small romaine lettuce

4 green onions, including unblemished green parts, trimmed and cut into diagonal slivers

24 fresh small mint leaves

¼ cup extra-virgin olive oil

1 teaspoon fresh lemon juice

Coarse sea salt and freshly ground pepper to taste

8 cherry tomatoes

8 Elitses or niçoise olives

4 ounces feta cheese, crumbled (about ⅔ cup)

Just before serving, stack the spinach and lettuce leaves and roll into a tight bundle; slice into ¼-inch-wide ribbons. In a shallow dish or salad bowl, combine the greens, green onions, and mint leaves.

Pour the olive oil over the greens and lightly toss everything together. Sprinkle with lemon juice, salt, and pepper. Scatter the tomatoes, olives, and feta cheese over.

WATERCRESS WITH PIQUANT CURRANT SAUCE

Watercress is abundant on Crete and features in many island recipes. Here, its bite is tempered by the fresh, clean flavor of lovage and combined with a sweet-sharp sauce of vinegar, honey, currants, and olive oil. Serve with full-flavored cheese and slices of pear, or with sausages, grilled meats, savory pies, or walnuts and olives.

Makes 8 meze, or 4 first-course or side-dish servings

2 tablespoons red wine vinegar

1 teaspoon Hymettus or other strongly flavored honey, or muscovado sugar

2 tablespoons dried currants

1 large bunch watercress, stemmed

¼ cup chopped fresh lovage, or ½ small stalk celery, finely diced

¼ cup extra-virgin olive oil

2 ripe pears, such as Bosc, Anjou, or Red Bartlett, peeled, cored, and cut into lengthwise slices

8 slices aged kephalotyri, aged graviera, or Italian pecorino cheese

Coarse sea salt and freshly ground pepper to taste

In a small nonreactive saucepan, combine the vinegar, honey, and currants. Heat over low heat until the honey or sugar is dissolved. Pour into a small bowl and set aside to cool completely.

In a medium bowl, combine the watercress and lovage or celery. Whisk the olive oil into the vinegar mixture. Pour the dressing over the greens and lightly toss.

Arrange the greens on one side of a platter, the pears and cheese on the other side. Sprinkle the greens with salt and pepper. Sprinkle the pears with pepper and serve.

A WARM SALAD OF BITTER GREENS

No authentic Greek meze table would be complete without a salad of lightly cooked wild greens (khorta). Depending on the season, I make this salad with young beet, dandelion, or turnip greens; radish tops; amaranth greens; or wild mustard, or sometimes with tender young greens I find in Chinese, Asian, or Middle Eastern markets.

Serve with salty meze delicacies like feta cheese, olives, sardines, or anchovies, or with fried or grilled foods.

Makes 8 meze, or 4 first-course or side-dish servings

$1\frac{1}{2}$ pounds greens such as beet, zucchini, dandelion, or turnip greens; radish tops; or amaranth or mustard greens, stemmed

$\frac{1}{2}$ cup water

1 tablespoon fresh lemon juice or red wine vinegar

$\frac{1}{4}$ cup extra-virgin olive oil

Coarse sea salt

Tear large leaves into smaller pieces. In a large, heavy nonreactive saucepan, bring the water to a boil. Add the greens and cover. Reduce heat to low and cook tender beet, zucchini, or dandelion greens for 1 to 2 minutes, turnip greens for 3 to 4 minutes, or amaranth or mustard for about 5 minutes, or until wilted and tender. Drain in a nonreactive colander, pressing on the greens with the back of a large wooden spoon to release the moisture.

Transfer the greens to a platter and loosen them with a fork. In a small bowl, whisk the lemon juice or vinegar and olive oil together. Pour the dressing over the greens. Sprinkle with salt. Serve warm or at room temperature.

MEZE BREAD SALAD

If "waste not, want not" is your motto, try this crunchy salad made with leftover bread. You'll have the basic ingredients in your pantry, and the vegetables can be varied according to what's in season.

This spring version is composed with fava beans, young carrots, artichoke hearts, and fresh herbs, but it also works well with tiny tomatoes, cucumber, and green onions, or with beets, green beans, and purslane or watercress. Assembled in minutes, versatile and packed with vitamins, it's an indispensable stand-by recipe.

Makes 8 meze or 2 light main-course servings

1 pound young fava beans, shelled

4 small, young carrots (about 6 ounces total), peeled and quartered lengthwise

Juice of ½ a small lemon

4 tablespoons extra-virgin olive oil, or to taste

Freshly ground pepper to taste

4 oil-packed artichoke hearts, drained and halved

8 Atalanti, Amfissa, or kalamata olives

2 tablespoons minced fresh dill, fennel fronds, or flat-leaf parsley

2 tablespoons snipped fresh chives

16 pieces Meze Breads (page 30)

4 ounces feta cheese or fresh white goat cheese, crumbled (about ⅔ cup)

Blanch the fava beans in boiling water for 2 minutes. Drain. Skin the beans by pulling off the skin and popping out each bean. Cook the carrots in a covered medium saucepan of simmering water for 6 minutes, or until just tender. Drain and set aside.

In a medium bowl, whisk together half the lemon juice, 2 tablespoons of the olive oil, and the pepper. Add the carrots, fava beans, and artichokes. Stir to coat all with the sauce. Cover and set aside for at least 1 hour or up to 3 hours.

Whisk together the remaining lemon juice and remaining 2 tablespoons olive oil and pour over the vegetables. Add the olives, dill (or fennel or parsley), and chives. Gently mix together, taking care not to break the vegetables. Combine with the meze bread and transfer everything to a shallow bowl or platter. Sprinkle with the cheese and serve.

LEMON-LACED ZUCCHINI WITH GREENS

This is the salad to make early in the season, whenever you find tiny young zucchini, sometimes with the flower still attached. Baked with olive oil and lemon, the zucchini are served with lightly cooked greens. This dish captures all the freshness and promise of early summer.

Good with baked or grilled fish or fried liver, or with Walnut-Garlic Sauce (page 110). Bake a few extra zucchini and use them to fill omelets or to serve with pasta.

Makes 8 meze or 4 side-dish servings

8 baby zucchini, 2 to 3 inches long

5 tablespoons extra-virgin olive oil

Juice of ½ a lemon

Coarse sea salt and freshly ground pepper to taste

1 to 2 tablespoons water

Large handful of young zucchini greens or pea shoots (you can find these in natural foods stores), or young dandelion or beet greens, stemmed

Lemon wedges for garnish

Preheat the oven to 375°F. Arrange the zucchini in a heavy, shallow baking dish just large enough to hold them in a single layer. Pour over 2 tablespoons of the olive oil and half the lemon juice. Sprinkle with salt and pepper. Add the water and lightly cover with aluminum foil. Bake for 5 minutes. Lower the oven temperature to 325°F. Continue baking for 20 to 30 minutes, or until the zucchini are just tender when pierced with a knife; roll them in the pan juices once or twice during baking, and add 1 or 2 tablespoons water to the dish if it appears dry. Set aside to cool.

Meanwhile, cook the greens in a covered steamer over rapidly simmering water for 4 minutes, or until just tender. Drain in a nonreactive colander, gently pressing on the greens with the back of a large wooden spoon to release the moisture.

Arrange the zucchini on one side of a platter and the greens on the other. Fork the greens to loosen the leaves. Whisk together the remaining 3 tablespoons olive oil and lemon juice and a few tablespoons of the pan juices. Pour this sauce over both zucchini and greens. Sprinkle with salt and pepper. Serve warm or at room temperature, with lemon wedges.

FRESH FAVA BEANS & FENNEL

In early spring, Greeks delight in the first fava beans. Heralding summer abundance, they bring freshness and flavor to the table and are enjoyed raw as café snacks or savored in simple meze dishes.

Here, the beans are cooked gently with olive oil and lemon juice, then coated in garlic, lemon, and olive oil and garnished with herbs. For a lunch or supper of perfect simplicity, team with goat cheese, country ham, black olives, and a glass or two of tsipouro or retsina.

Makes 8 meze or 4 first-course servings

2 pounds young fava beans (choose unblemished pods, see page 120)

5 tablespoons extra-virgin olive oil

3 tablespoons fresh lemon juice

2 tablespoons water

1 small clove garlic, minced

Coarse sea salt and freshly ground pepper to taste

2 tablespoons chopped fresh fennel fronds, dill, or flat-leaf parsley

8 small green onions, including best green parts

8 radishes, fresh young leaves intact

Shell the fava beans. In a medium saucepan of boiling water, blanch the shelled beans for 2 minutes; drain.

Pull off the skin and pop out each jade-green bean.

In a heavy skillet over low heat, heat 2½ tablespoons of the olive oil. Add the beans, 1 tablespoon of the lemon juice, and the water. Reduce heat to very low, cover, and cook the fava beans for 2 minutes, or until just tender. Using a slotted spoon, transfer the beans to a bowl and set aside; reserve the pan juices.

In a mortar or small bowl, combine the garlic, salt, and pepper. Using a pestle or wooden spoon, pound to a paste. Whisk in the remaining 2 tablespoons lemon juice and 2½ tablespoons olive oil, then whisk in the pan juices. Pour this sauce over the beans; stir to mix. Taste and adjust the seasoning. Transfer to a platter and sprinkle with the herb. Surround with the green onions and radishes. Serve within 1 hour.

KOS LENTILS & OLIVES

This is a new take on a popular dish from the island of Kos. Sun-dried tomatoes or roasted red bell pepper is substituted for the traditional sweet-spiced preserved tomatoes. The earthy taste of the lentils is offset by olives, green onions, a robust dressing, and fresh cilantro and parsley. Serve with grilled meats or as a light lunch with good bread, slices of cheese, and a green salad.

Makes 8 meze or 4 side-dish servings

1 cup green lentils, picked over and rinsed

1 salt-packed anchovy fillet, rinsed, soaked, and patted dry (see page 118)

Pinch of ground allspice

¼ teaspoon coarsely ground pepper

2 tablespoons minced fresh flat-leaf parsley

1 tablespoon red wine vinegar

¼ cup extra-virgin olive oil

12 Thasos olives or other salt- or brine-cured black olives, pitted and quartered

2 green onions, including best green parts, cut into diagonal slivers

¼ cup coarsely chopped fresh cilantro

2 oil-packed sun-dried tomatoes, drained and cut into thin strips

Coarse sea salt to taste

Put the lentils in a saucepan, add water to cover by 2 inches, and bring to a boil over medium heat. Reduce heat to low, cover, and simmer for 15 to 20 minutes, or until just tender. Drain, and set aside to cool.

In a mortar or small bowl, combine the anchovy, allspice, pepper, and parsley and pound to mix with a pestle or wooden spoon. Add the vinegar and continue pounding until the anchovy disintegrates. Whisk in the olive oil. In a large bowl, combine the lentils and olive oil mixture. Add the olives, green onions, cilantro, and tomatoes. Sprinkle with salt. To serve, transfer to a platter or shallow bowl.

PEPPERY CHEESE SALAD

This mountain salad combines peppery watercress with feta or goat cheese and a fruity olive oil dressing. Serve this right after you make it, so that no flavor or crispness is lost, with black olives and salted toasted almonds (see below). It's also a lively filling for whole-wheat sandwiches or a spread for rye or salt-free crackers.

The best thing about this salad is its versatility. I like the following simple olive oil version best and serve it on painted earthenware to show off its pleasing whiteness blushed with paprika and cayenne. But you can also add herbs or olives, pickled peppers, radishes, and/or garlic to the basic cheese mixture for variety of taste and texture.

Makes 8 meze or 4 first-course servings

½ cup crumbled feta cheese or fresh white goat cheese (about 2½ ounces)

1 cup cottage cheese, drained

¼ teaspoon finely cracked pepper

3 tablespoons extra-virgin olive oil

2 slices whole-wheat bread, toasted

1 small bunch watercress, stemmed

8 Amfissa, Atalanti, or kalamata olives

1 red bell pepper, roasted, peeled, and cut into thin strips (see page 123)

Squeeze of fresh lemon juice

¼ teaspoon paprika

Pinch of cayenne pepper

In a medium bowl, combine the feta or goat and cottage cheeses. Sprinkle with the pepper and stir until well mixed. Stir in ½ tablespoon of the olive oil. Spread over a platter. Cut the crusts from the toast and cut each slice into 4 triangles. Surround the cheese mixture with the watercress and toast triangles. Heap the olives and bell pepper to one side of the cheese.

Whisk the lemon juice and remaining 2½ tablespoons olive oil together. Sprinkle half this sauce over the bread, watercress, and bell pepper. Whisk the paprika and cayenne into the remaining sauce and sprinkle this over the cheese. Serve immediately.

SALTED TOASTED ALMONDS: Combine 1 cup unblanched almonds with 2 tablespoons fresh lemon juice, mix well, and set aside for 15 minutes. Spread in one layer on a baking sheet and sprinkle with 1 tablespoon coarse sea salt. Place on the top shelf of a preheated 325°F oven and bake 10 to 12 minutes, or until the almonds are crisp and beginning to brown. Let cool before storing in a covered container for up to 4 weeks.

HOT PLATES & SAVORY PIES

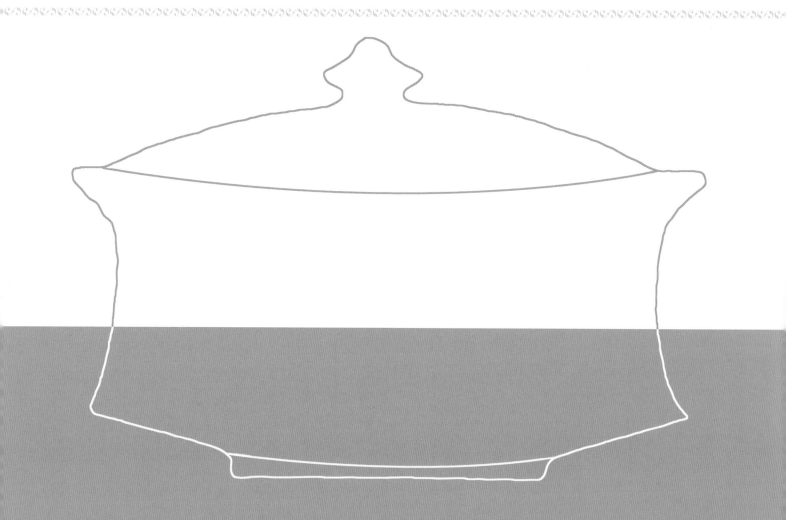

Daring and surprise are the hallmarks of hot mezes. They are often spiced—with cinnamon, coriander, pepper, or sesame—or heavily fragranced with bay leaves, Greek oregano, rosemary, and parsley. Sometimes they startle with an unexpected yoking together of contrasting ingredients, tastes, and textures, mixing sweet with tart, subtle with explosive, coarse with smooth.

The meze table is never dominated by these hot dishes. Just one or two skillfully chosen and executed examples act as a counterpoint to the other dishes. To my mind the effect is like that produced by simultaneously striking different musical notes: There is individual character but a satisfying harmony overall.

For a quick and easy-to-assemble meze table, make one or two hot dishes from this chapter and serve with well-flavored olives, cheeses, nuts, and perhaps a dish of greens. There's economy here, too: Some dishes make good use of leftover cooked meat, chicken, fish, or vegetables, while others feature inexpensive fish or variety meats. One or two are very simple to make at the very last minute.

The savory pies of the meze table deserve special mention. These melting rolls, squares, or triangles of light-as-a-feather pastry conceal cheese, meat, or vegetables. Bite-sized and highly flavored, these tiny pies disappear in seconds, and few guests can resist them for long. Best of all, although they look impressively intricate and time-consuming, they are really very easy to make with a little practice.

FISH ON A TILE

In this Macedonian recipe, a long, curved roof tile makes an efficient baking dish for marinated fish. Any fish can be cooked this way, but firm-fleshed, fatty fish work particularly well. Use a glazed earthenware dish to replace the tile.

This is definitely a dish for garlic lovers, but the garlic is tempered by the addition of rosemary sprigs and lemon pieces to make a dish with all the sunshine taste of a Greek summer. Serve with khorta (see page 122) or a green salad, black olives, and a dry red wine.

Makes 8 meze or 4 first-course servings

12 ounces bonito, mackerel, or tuna fillets

Coarse sea salt and freshly ground pepper to taste

¼ teaspoon paprika

6 tablespoons extra-virgin olive oil

8 cloves garlic

6 sprigs rosemary, plus more for garnish

1 organic lemon, halved, cut into large pieces, and seeded

2 slices country-style bread, toasted

Put the fillets in a bowl and sprinkle with salt, pepper, paprika, and 2 tablespoons of the olive oil; turn the fish to coat in this marinade. Cover and set aside.

Put a heavy baking dish, large enough to hold the fish and garlic cloves in one layer, in the oven and preheat the oven to 300°F.

Trim off a thin slice from the stem end of each garlic clove and rub off the feathery outer skins with your fingers. Pour the remaining 4 tablespoons olive oil into the baking dish and put the garlic cloves, 6 rosemary sprigs, and the lemon pieces in it. Bake, uncovered, for 40 minutes, basting the garlic and lemon pieces once or twice.

Push the garlic and lemon pieces to one side of the dish and arrange the fillets in it in a single layer. Pour over any marinade and baste with the hot olive oil. Increase the oven temperature to 325°F. Bake, uncovered, for 15 to 20 minutes, or until the fillets are just opaque throughout.

Transfer the fish to a warm platter or individual plates. Cut the crusts from the toast and cut the toast into 8 triangles. Surround the fish with the bread. Discard the rosemary sprigs. With a wooden spoon, crush the lemon pieces into the hot oil to release as much juice as possible (don't worry if some of the flesh separates out, too). Discard the lemons. Taste and adjust the seasoning of the pan juices. Pour the juices over the fish and bread. With the back of a knife, gently squeeze the garlic pulp out of the cloves onto the bread. Garnish with rosemary sprigs and serve warm.

TUNA IN ANCHOVY-CAPER SAUCE

Tuna has a rich meatiness and an assertive taste that works well with other strong flavors. Scented and spiced by a tangy marinade, here it is served with a traditional sauce of anchovies, capers, and bay leaves. Serve with khorta (see page 122), olives, Meze Breads (page 30), and graviera, kephalotyri, or Italian pecorino cheese.

Makes 8 meze or 4 first-course servings

1½ tablespoons red wine vinegar

Large pinch of paprika

8 tablespoons extra-virgin olive oil

12 ounces fresh tuna fillets, cut into 8 pieces

3 sprigs flat-leaf parsley

6 bay leaves

1 clove garlic, minced

2 salt-packed anchovy fillets, rinsed, soaked, patted dry, and chopped (see page 118)

1 tablespoon dried Greek oregano or rigani

1 generous tablespoon salt-packed small capers, soaked, rinsed, and patted dry (see page 118)

Finely cracked pepper to taste

Small purslane or watercress sprigs for garnish

In a small bowl, whisk together 1 tablespoon of the vinegar, the paprika, and 3 tablespoons of the olive oil. Rub each piece of tuna with this marinade. In a shallow bowl, arrange the fish in 2 layers, with the parsley sprigs and bay leaves tucked between the layers. Pour over any remaining marinade. Cover and set aside in a cool place for at least 1 hour or up to 2 hours.

In a small saucepan over very low heat, heat 4 tablespoons of the olive oil and cook the garlic for a minute or two until fragrant. Add the anchovies and oregano. Remove from heat. With a pestle or wooden spoon, mash the anchovies until they disintegrate; set the pan aside.

Heat a large, heavy skillet over medium-low heat until hot. Remove the parsley and bay leaves from the tuna. Brush the skillet with the remaining 1 tablespoon olive oil and lightly sear the tuna on both sides. Reduce heat to low and continue cooking, turning once with a spatula, until the fish is still slightly translucent in the center, 2 to 3 minutes.

Add the remaining ½ tablespoon vinegar, the capers, and any pan juices to the anchovy sauce. Return the pan to low heat and heat to warm, stirring once or twice. Arrange the fish on a platter and pour the anchovy sauce over. Sprinkle with pepper and surround with purslane or watercress. Serve warm or at room temperature.

LITTLE FISH FRITTERS

No visitor to Greece forgets his or her first taste of a meze platter piled high with tiny golden fish fritters. This is not a dish for formal entertaining, but a treat to share with friends in the kitchen, eating straight from the pan.

The fish can be tiny whole anchovies or whitebait, shelled mussels, shrimp or prawns, or bite-sized pieces of eel, bonito, or mackerel, but it must be really fresh. The secret of the light-as-a-whisper batter is a dash of frothy beer and an overnight rest in the refrigerator. Serve with Watercress with Piquant Currant Sauce (page 63).

Makes 8 meze or 4 first-course servings

BATTER

1 egg white

¼ cup garbanzo bean flour

¼ cup all-purpose flour

Fine sea salt and freshly ground
     pepper to taste

¼ cup beer, or enough to make
     a batter

24 tiny (1 to 2 inches long) fresh fish
     such as anchovies or whitebait, or
     1 pound boneless, skinless eel,
     mackerel, or bonito, cut into 16
     bite-sized pieces

Olive oil for frying

1 tablespoon dried Greek oregano or
     rigani, crumbled

Coarse sea salt and freshly ground
     pepper to taste

Lemon wedges for garnish

To make the batter: In a medium bowl, whisk the egg white until soft peaks form. Sift in the garbanzo bean flour, all-purpose flour, salt, and pepper. Stir to mix. Stir in enough beer to make a batter the consistency of pouring cream. Cover and refrigerate overnight.

Remove the batter from the refrigerator and whisk well. Rinse the fish and dry with paper towels.

Pour a ¼-inch layer of olive oil into a large, heavy skillet set over medium-low heat. Heat until hot but not smoking (a little batter will sizzle immediately when added). Hold 2 or 3 tiny fish together by their tails and dip them into the batter, or dip the fish pieces into the batter, one at a time. Use a slotted spoon to transfer the fish to the skillet; don't overcrowd. Fry until golden brown, turning once; lightly flatten each fritter with a spatula to cook evenly. Using the slotted spoon, transfer to paper towels to drain. Repeat with the remaining fritters.

Pile the fritters on a warmed platter. Sprinkle with the oregano, salt, and pepper. Surround with lemon wedges and serve immediately.

SIPHNOS SHRIMP KEPHTEDES WITH CUCUMBER SALAD

These patties from Siphnos look pretty and taste sublime. To the sea-freshness of shrimp is added green onion, aged cheese, dill, and parsley. The result is a delicate flavor and a satisfying, crunchy texture.

For convenience, you can prepare these ahead of time. They're even more scrumptious with Green Olive Sauce (page 56).

Makes 8 meze or 4 first-course servings

12 ounces small shrimp, shelled

2 tablespoons extra-virgin olive oil, plus more for frying

2 green onions, white parts only, finely chopped

2 tablespoons finely grated aged graviera, aged kephalotyri, or Italian pecorino cheese

3 tablespoons brown rice flakes, lightly pulverized in a mortar, or coarse fresh whole-wheat bread crumbs, lightly toasted (see page 118)

¼ cup minced fresh flat-leaf parsley

1 tablespoon minced fresh dill

Sea salt and freshly ground pepper to taste

1 egg, beaten

½ English (hothouse) cucumber, peeled and cut into fine dice

½ small red onion, finely chopped

½ teaspoon sumac, or large pinch of paprika

Lemon wedges for garnish

Rinse the shrimp and spread on paper towels to dry. In a large, heavy skillet over low heat, heat the 2 tablespoons olive oil and cook the shrimp, stirring once or twice, for about 4 minutes, or until evenly pink. Chop ¼ cup of the shrimp into fine dice and mince the remainder.

In a large bowl, combine the diced and minced shrimp, green onions, cheese, rice flakes or bread crumbs, 1 tablespoon of the parsley, the dill, salt, and pepper. Add the egg and stir to mix. Cover and refrigerate for 1 to 2 hours.

With your hands, shape the shrimp mixture into 8 balls and slightly flatten each one to make a patty. In a large, heavy skillet over medium-low heat, heat a thin layer of olive oil and sauté the patties on both sides until pale golden brown. Using a slotted spoon, transfer to paper towels to drain.

Meanwhile, combine the cucumber, red onion, the remaining parsley, and the sumac or paprika in a small bowl. Add salt and pepper to taste and toss. Heap the salad along one side of a platter. Arrange the patties alongside and garnish with lemon wedges. Serve warm or at room temperature.

BAY-SCENTED MARINATED CHICKEN

This glossy sweet-sour dish of chicken with currants shows off flavor notes that take us back to antiquity: bay leaf, parsley, olive oil, vinegar, and honey. But there's nothing ancient about its convenience and appeal. It is simple to prepare and serve, and it looks mouthwateringly appetizing on a buffet table. Serve with A Warm Salad of Bitter Greens (page 64) or a green salad, Yogurt Cheese (page 18), and other vegetable dishes.

Makes 8 meze or 4 light main-course servings

4 skinless, boneless chicken breast halves

2 tablespoons red wine vinegar

½ teaspoon ground coriander

4 tablespoons extra-virgin olive oil, plus more for brushing

8 bay leaves

4 sprigs flat-leaf parsley

1 teaspoon Hymettus or other strongly flavored honey

2 tablespoons water

¼ cup dried currants or small dark seedless raisins

Coarse sea salt and freshly ground pepper to taste

Elitses or niçoise olives, drained and rinsed, for garnish

Cut each chicken breast into 2 crosswise pieces and put them in a shallow bowl. Whisk 1 tablespoon of the vinegar, the coriander, and 2 tablespoons of the olive oil together and pour over the chicken pieces; turn to coat. Push 4 of the bay leaves and the parsley sprigs between the chicken pieces. Cover and set aside for 2 hours.

Choose a shallow baking dish just large enough to comfortably hold the chicken pieces in a single layer. Place it in the oven and preheat the oven to 350°F.

Brush the dish with olive oil. Discard the parsley sprigs and transfer the chicken, bay leaves, and marinade to the dish. Whisk together the remaining 1 tablespoon vinegar and the honey, then whisk in the remaining 2 tablespoons olive oil. Add this sauce to the dish with the water, the remaining bay leaves, the currants or raisins, salt, and pepper. Bake, uncovered, for 15 minutes, then baste the chicken. Cover the dish with aluminum foil and bake 10 to 15 minutes longer, or until the chicken is opaque throughout. Add the olives and bake for 5 more minutes.

Arrange the chicken pieces on a warmed platter and pour the pan juices, currants, bay leaves, and olives over. Serve hot or warm.

HONEY-CHICKEN KEPHTEDES

The flavors of these crisp, savory-sweet patties reflect Greece's ancient culinary past. The sweetness of honey and prunes is balanced by an acidic red wine vinegar bite. Chopped walnuts add crunch, and thyme or fennel adds pungency. This is a useful recipe for turning leftover chicken into a delicious lunch dish, too.

Makes 8 meze or 4 first-course servings

1 tablespoon Hymettus or other strongly flavored honey

2 tablespoons red wine vinegar, or 1 tablespoon balsamic vinegar combined with 1 tablespoon water

8 ounces cooked chicken, finely diced (about 1¼ cups)

3 prunes, pitted and finely chopped

3 walnuts, broken into small pieces, or ¼ cup pine nuts, toasted and chopped (see page 124)

½ tablespoon dried thyme, crumbled, or 2 tablespoons minced fresh fennel fronds

2 tablespoons minced fresh chives or green onion leaves

Coarse sea salt and freshly ground pepper to taste

1 egg, lightly beaten

2 tablespoons chicken broth, or 1 tablespoon extra-virgin olive oil

3 tablespoons brown rice flakes, crumbled, or coarse fresh whole-wheat bread crumbs, lightly toasted (see page 118)

Extra-virgin olive oil for frying, plus 2 tablespoons

Large handful of mixed greens such as watercress, cilantro, and/or flat-leaf parsley sprigs, mâche, frisée, arugula, and/or purslane

½ tablespoon fresh lemon juice

Elitses or niçoise olives, drained, for garnish

In a large bowl, combine the honey and vinegar. Add the chicken and stir to coat. With a fork, mix in the prunes, walnuts, thyme or fennel, chives or green onion, salt, and pepper. Whisk together the egg, broth or olive oil, and rice flakes or bread crumbs. Lightly combine with the chicken mixture. Cover and refrigerate for 1 or 2 hours to chill.

Shape the chicken mixture into 8 balls and slightly flatten each one between your palms to make a patty.

In a large, heavy skillet over medium-low heat, heat a thin layer of olive oil and sauté the patties on both sides until a light golden brown. Using a slotted metal spatula, transfer to paper towels to drain.

Arrange the greens on one side of a platter. In a small bowl, whisk the lemon juice and the 2 tablespoons olive oil together. Pour over the greens and sprinkle with salt and pepper. Arrange the patties alongside. Serve warm or hot, with olives.

ROSY LAMB

Fast cooking is the key to tender meat in this tasty dish. The honey-sweetened sauce, based on sun-dried tomatoes and spiced with cinnamon, is wonderfully adaptable and may also be used on chicken, shellfish, fish, and steamed or fried zucchini or cauliflower.

Makes 8 meze or 4 light main-course servings

8 tiny lamb chops, or 1 pound lamb tenderloin

2 tablespoons extra-virgin olive oil

Coarse sea salt and freshly ground pepper to taste

8 bay leaves

SPICY TOMATO SAUCE

3 oil-packed sun-dried tomatoes, drained and diced

1 clove garlic, chopped

½ teaspoon Hymettus or other strongly flavored honey

Large pinch of ground cinnamon

3 tablespoons minced fresh flat-leaf parsley

½ tablespoon fresh lemon juice

4 tablespoons extra-virgin olive oil

2 tablespoons beef broth, vegetable broth, or water

1 tablespoon fresh lemon juice

16 Elitses or niçoise olives

Trim off any fat from the lamb chops, or cut the tenderloin into 8 crosswise pieces, then tie each piece into a medallion with a piece of kitchen string. Rub the meat with the olive oil. Sprinkle with salt and pepper. Put in a bowl with the bay leaves. Cover and set aside for at least 1 hour or up to 2 hours.

Discard the bay leaves. Heat a heavy skillet over medium-low heat and add the meat and marinade. Sauté the meat on both sides for about 10 minutes, or until well browned.

While the meat is cooking, make the sauce: In a food processor, combine the tomatoes, garlic, honey, cinnamon, 2 tablespoons parsley, ½ tablespoon lemon juice, and olive oil. Process until smooth; don't worry if the oil separates. Transfer to a small saucepan and gently heat to warm.

Push the meat to one side of the skillet with a spoon and reduce heat to low. Add the broth or water and 1 tablespoon lemon juice. Stir to scrape up any browned bits from the bottom of the pan.

Spread the tomato sauce over the platter. Arrange the meat on top and pour the pan juices over. Sprinkle with pepper to taste and the remaining parsley. Serve warm, with olives.

COUNTRY SAUSAGES

This homey farmhouse dish of sliced sausage and potato is cooked in olive oil and served on a bed of greens. What makes it a memorable meze is just the right amount of coriander and cumin to spice up the sausages, and dashes of lively mustard and red wine vinegar to lift the sauce.

Makes 8 meze or 2 main-course servings

6 small potatoes (about 8 ounces total), scrubbed

5 tablespoons extra-virgin olive oil

8 ounces homemade or good-quality commercial sausages, cut into ½-inch crosswise slices

½ tablespoon ground coriander

½ teaspoon ground cumin

Coarsely ground pepper to taste

Large handful of beet greens, broccoli rabe, amaranth, or other greens (see page 122), leaves stripped from coarse stalks and well rinsed

1 tablespoon red wine vinegar

1 teaspoon Meaux mustard, or ½ teaspoon Dijon mustard mixed with a few drops of honey

Coarse sea salt to taste

Cook the potatoes in salted boiling water for 12 minutes, or until just tender. Drain and cut into halves.

In a large, heavy skillet over low heat, heat 2 tablespoons of the olive oil and sauté the sausage slices on both sides for about 6 minutes, or until they release some of their fat; don't let them brown. Mix the coriander, cumin, and pepper together and sprinkle over the sausages; turn the sausages in the olive oil. Add the potatoes and, with a spatula or fork, evenly space the pieces among the sausages; continue cooking and turning for about 8 minutes, or until both sausages and potatoes are lightly browned on all sides.

Meanwhile, place a large, heavy saucepan over low heat and add the greens. Cover and cook for 1 to 2 minutes, or until just tender, stirring once or twice with a wooden spoon. Drain in a colander and press the greens against the sides with the back of the spoon to extract as much moisture as possible. With a large knife, coarsely chop the greens and keep them warm.

In a small bowl, mix the vinegar and mustard together. Stir in the remaining 3 tablespoons olive oil.

Fork the greens over a warmed platter, pour the sauce over, and sprinkle with salt and pepper to taste. Arrange the sausages and potatoes on top and serve immediately.

SFONGATA

Sfongata *is similar to a frittata. The word means "sponge,"
which perfectly describes the light, airy texture of this
country egg dish. Fillings vary according to the season, but
what's really important is the quality of the ingredients:
very fresh eggs, crisp vegetables, fragrant herbs, and a
pungent olive oil. Served with a green salad or cooked
greens, olives, and crusty bread, sfongata makes a quick
lunch or supper.*

Makes 8 meze or 2 light main-course servings

2 zucchini (about 6 ounces total),
scrubbed and trimmed

Coarse sea salt to taste

3 tablespoons extra-virgin olive oil

2 heaped tablespoons diced lean
pancetta, speck, or prosciutto

Freshly ground pepper to taste

2 tablespoons unsalted butter

½ cup coarse fresh whole-wheat
bread crumbs

2 ounces feta cheese, crumbled
(about ⅓ cup)

3 eggs, well beaten

3 tablespoons snipped fresh chives

2 tablespoons coarsely chopped
fresh flat-leaf parsley or chervil

Lemon wedges for garnish

Elitses or niçoise olives for garnish

Cut the zucchini into matchsticks with a knife, or use the
julienne blade on a mandoline or food processor. Sprinkle
with salt and set aside for 30 minutes to 1 hour.

In a 10-inch omelet pan or skillet over low heat, heat
2 tablespoons of the olive oil and sauté the pancetta for
4 minutes, or until starting to crisp; cook speck or prosciutto
for 1 minute only, to flavor the oil. Using a slotted spoon,
transfer to paper towels to drain. Add the remaining 1 tablespoon olive oil to the pan. Gently but firmly squeeze the
zucchini slices between paper towels to remove as much
water as possible. Add the zucchini to the pan; separate the
slices with a fork, and spread evenly over the base of the
pan. Sprinkle with pepper and cook for 5 to 8 minutes,
or until the zucchini just begin to turn gold. Using a slotted
spoon, transfer to a plate.

Add the butter to the pan and swirl it around. Sprinkle the
bread crumbs over the base of the pan and cook, stirring
once or twice, for 3 to 4 minutes, or until pale golden.
Sprinkle the pancetta speck, or prosciutto and feta over,
then fork the zucchini over to make an even layer, disturb-
ing the bread crumbs as little as possible.

(continued on page 88)

Increase the heat under the pan to medium-low. Pour in the eggs and gently tilt the pan to spread evenly. Sprinkle with 2 tablespoons of the chives, 1 tablespoon of the parsley, and salt and pepper to taste. Cook for 1 to 2 minutes, or until lightly browned underneath; gently shake the pan once or twice. Cover the sfongata with an inverted plate, hold it firmly in place, and invert both so the sfongata is upside down on the plate. Slide it back into the pan and continue cooking until lightly browned on the second side.

Invert a serving plate over the pan and turn out the sfongata so the zucchini is uppermost; sprinkle with the remaining chives and parsley. Cut into 8 or 2 slices and serve warm, with lemon wedges and olives.

VARIATION: Try other fillings, too: Lightly sauté a handful of greens such as beet greens or spinach, or a few blanched leaves of tender greens, asparagus, artichoke hearts, or sliced mushrooms tossed in olive oil, before adding the eggs. Or, try a more substantial filling of sliced sausage or sautéed lamb's kidney and diced potato; lightly brown both meat and potato before adding the eggs.

Diced sweet tomatoes are another traditional filling, but this softer version of sfongata can be difficult to successfully turn; instead, gently cook the sfongata without turning, until the eggs are creamy, then place under a hot broiler for barely 1 minute, or until the eggs are set. Scatter tiny black olives and aromatic herbs over before serving.

EGGPLANTS IN SPICY TOMATO-PARSLEY SAUCE

I love the sweet spiciness of this popular meze, a legacy from the Turkish invasion of Greece in medieval times. The tiny eggplants, split to tuck in garlic, cumin, and parsley, are cooked whole and served with an aromatic honey-sweetened onion and tomato sauce.

This is a recipe to reach for when you are planning a party—it's easy to make in large quantities, it can be made ahead of time, and it can be served at any temperature. Accompany with sausages or grilled mezes and a chunk of tasty bread for a satisfying lunch.

Makes 8 meze or 4 first-course servings

16 baby eggplants, each about 2 inches long, stemmed and rinsed

6 tablespoons extra-virgin olive oil

1 tablespoon cumin seeds, or 1 teaspoon ground cumin

1 clove garlic, minced

Coarse sea salt to taste

½ teaspoon freshly ground pepper, or to taste

Small handful of fresh flat-leaf parsley leaves, coarsely chopped

1 onion, finely chopped

1 pound tomatoes, peeled, cored, and diced (juices reserved)

1 teaspoon honey

Leaves from 4 sprigs mint

With the point of a paring knife, make an incision through to the center of each eggplant and along most of its length. In a heavy skillet over medium-low heat, heat 3 tablespoons of the olive oil until hot but not smoking and sauté the eggplants on all sides for about 10 minutes, or until the skins are a little shriveled. Using a slotted spoon, transfer to paper towels to drain. Wipe the skillet with more paper towels.

Pulverize the cumin seeds in a mortar or grinder. In a small, dry skillet over very low heat, heat the ground cumin until fragrant. With a large knife, chop the garlic, salt, cumin, ¼ teaspoon of the pepper, and half the parsley together. Gently ease open each eggplant incision and, with a small spoon, fill with the parsley mixture.

Return the first skillet to low heat, add the remaining 3 tablespoons olive oil, and sauté the onion until soft, about 8 minutes. Add the tomatoes and their juice, the honey, salt to taste, and the remaining ¼ teaspoon pepper, and simmer, stirring occasionally, for 20 minutes or until thickened.

Carefully transfer the eggplants to the sauce and add half the remaining parsley. Cover the skillet and, holding the lid in place, shake gently to mix everything together. Reduce heat to very low and simmer for 15 minutes. Add a few tablespoons of water if the sauce appears too dry. Taste and adjust the seasoning; the sauce should be highly flavored.

Tear the mint leaves into pieces and lightly chop together with the remaining parsley. Transfer the eggplants to a warm platter, pour the sauce over, and sprinkle with the mint mixture.

SESAME LEEKS

Leeks have a chameleonlike quality, managing to blend beautifully with strong flavors while holding onto their essential character. Here, they are gently baked in a sauce of red wine vinegar, honey, and bay leaves, to which is added a sweet sesame spiciness. Serve this elegant dish with grilled foods or small pies (pages 98 and 101) and cooked greens.

Makes 8 meze or 4 first-course servings

8   slender (½-inch-wide) leeks, or 16 large, plump green onions

¼   cup chicken broth, vegetable broth, or hot water

2   tablespoons extra-virgin olive oil

2   tablespoons sesame seeds, lightly toasted (see page 125)

8   bay leaves

½   tablespoon Hymettus or other strongly flavored honey

1   tablespoon red wine vinegar, or ½ tablespoon balsamic vinegar

1   tablespoon sesame oil or extra-virgin olive oil

Coarse sea salt and freshly ground pepper to taste

8   ounces aged kephalotyri, aged graviera, or Italian pecorino cheese, cut into 8 or 16 slices

Trim most of the green from the leeks or any blemished green parts from the green onions. Slice each leek lengthwise into the center, gently ease the layers open with your fingers, and hold the leek upright under cold running water until the water runs clear.

Preheat the oven to 325°F. In an ovenproof sauté pan or skillet large enough to hold the leeks or green onions in a single layer, bring 1 inch water to a boil. Add the leeks or green onions, reduce heat, cover, and simmer leeks for 5 minutes, green onions for 1 minute; turn once. Drain and rinse under cold running water.

Shake off the excess water and arrange the leeks or green onions in a shallow, heavy baking dish just large enough to hold them in a single layer. Pour the broth or water and olive oil over, sprinkle with sesame seeds, and put 4 of the bay leaves in the dish. Cover with a lid or aluminum foil and bake leeks for 25 minutes, green onions for 10 to 15 minutes, or until tender when pierced with a knife. Add 1 or 2 tablespoons of water to the dish if the sauce appears to be less than ⅓ cup.

Arrange the leeks or green onions and bay leaves on a warmed platter. Pour the pan juices into a small bowl. Whisk in the honey, vinegar, sesame or olive oil, salt, and pepper. Pour over the leeks. Garnish with the remaining 4 bay leaves, surround with the cheese, and serve warm or at room temperature.

CINNAMON-CHEESE PIES

In traditional Cretan kitchens, the pastry for these plump pies is flavored with orange juice. The pies are either shaped into squares with the filling partly exposed and baked, or into closed squares and half moons and fried. The filling is ricotta and feta cheeses flavored with honey and mint; after baking, the pies are dusted with sugar and cinnamon. A delightful snack anytime, especially with a bowl of honey and a sweet Samos wine, these pies are also good accompaniments to Eggplants in Spicy Tomato-Parsley Sauce (page 89) or Peppered Greek Oregano Pork (page 100), A Warm Salad of Bitter Greens (page 64), and a full-bodied rosé wine.

Makes 8 small or 16 tiny pies; 8 meze or 4 side-dish servings

PASTRY

2 cups unbleached all-purpose flour

1 teaspoon sea salt

½ teaspoon superfine sugar

2 egg whites

¼ cup strained fresh orange juice

3 tablespoons extra-virgin olive oil

FILLING

1 cup ricotta cheese or small-curd cottage cheese, drained for 15 minutes

½ cup (3 ounces) grated feta cheese

1 tablespoon Hymettus or other strongly flavored honey

1 tablespoon dried mint, crumbled

Olive oil for brushing

3 tablespoons water

1 egg yolk

1½ tablespoons confectioners' sugar

1 scant teaspoon ground cinnamon

TO MAKE THE PASTRY: Sift the flour, salt, and sugar into a large bowl. In a medium bowl, whisk the egg whites until soft peaks form. Stir into the flour with the orange juice and olive oil. Transfer to a lightly floured board and knead for 5 to 10 minutes. Be patient; for the first few minutes of kneading, the dough will appear dry. Tightly wrap in plastic wrap and refrigerate for 1 hour.

TO MAKE THE FILLING: In a medium bowl, combine the ricotta cheese, feta cheese, honey, and mint. Set aside.

Preheat the oven to 350°F. Liberally brush a heavy baking sheet with olive oil. Remove the dough from the refrigerator and divide in half. Rewrap one portion and refrigerate it. Roll the dough out as thin as possible.

(continued on page 94)

TO MAKE SQUARE PIES WITH FILLING ENCLOSED:
Cut the pastry into four 6-by-3-inch rectangles or eight
4-by-2-inch rectangles. Place one-eighth (or one-sixteenth)
of the filling in the center of one half of each rectangle.
Dip your finger in 2 tablespoons of the water and run it
along the pastry edges to lightly dampen. Fold over to make
squares, and seal by crimping the edges with a pastry wheel
or fork. To make square pies with a little filling exposed:
Cut the pastry into four 3-by-3-inch squares, or eight 2-by-
2-inch squares. Place one-eighth (or one-sixteenth) of the
filling in the center of each square. Pull the corners of each
square almost to the center and press the 4 edges up and
together, leaving a little filling exposed.

Place the pies 1 inch apart on the baking sheet and repeat
with the remaining pastry and filling. Liberally brush the
pies with olive oil and bake for 10 minutes, or until the pastry is set. Whisk 1 tablespoon water into the egg yolk and
brush the pastries with this glaze. Bake 10 to 15 minutes
longer, or until golden brown.

Just before serving, combine the confectioners' sugar and
cinnamon and dust the pies with this mixture.

VARIATION: You can use the same pastry and filling to
make half-moon pies (Savory Honey-Pear Pies, page 96), or
use the filling in Feta & Lamb Pies (page 101).

GREENS & GARBANZO BEAN FRITTERS

These cumin-spiced fritters can be infinitely varied according to the herbs and vegetables available. This spring version teams garbanzo beans with wild greens and fresh herbs. The fritters can be made with other vegetables, herbs, and seasonings, or sweetened with raisins or prunes and walnuts.

Beet or amaranth greens, which retain their flavor and shape during cooking, work best here. Avoid canned garbanzo beans, which are too soft and lacking in flavor to produce the right texture and taste. Serve warm or at room temperature, with olives and yogurt.

Makes 16 fritters; 8 meze or 4 first-course servings

½ cup dried garbanzo beans

1 cinnamon stick, broken into 2 pieces

2 bay leaves

Large handful of young, fresh beet greens or red chard, stripped from coarse stalks

1 tablespoon fresh lemon juice

2 eggs

5 tablespoons garbanzo bean flour or whole-wheat flour

1 teaspoon cumin seeds, toasted and ground (see page 125)

¼ teaspoon paprika

Sea salt and freshly ground pepper to taste

2 tablespoons minced fresh fennel fronds, dill, or flat-leaf parsley

Extra-virgin olive oil for frying

1 teaspoon sumac, or ¼ teaspoon paprika

Lemon wedges for garnish

Rinse and pick over the beans. Soak overnight in cold water to cover by 2 inches. Drain the beans, rinse well, and put in a saucepan with cold water to cover by 3 inches. Add the cinnamon stick and bay leaves. Bring to a boil, reduce heat to low, cover, and simmer for about 40 minutes, or until tender. Drain, discard the cinnamon stick and bay leaves, and set aside.

Put the greens in a large, heavy saucepan. Cover and cook over low heat for about 3 minutes, or until wilted, stirring once or twice. Drain and squeeze dry with paper towels. With a large knife, coarsely chop the greens. Sprinkle with the lemon juice and set aside.

In a food processor or a mortar, mash the beans to a coarse paste. In a large bowl, whisk the eggs until light and frothy. Whisk in 3 tablespoons of the flour, the cumin, paprika, salt, and pepper. Stir in the bean paste, greens, and fennel fronds or herb. Divide the mixture into 16 portions and slightly flatten each to make a fritter. Dust a board or plate with 1 tablespoon of the flour, lay the fritters on it, and dust with the remaining 1 tablespoon flour.

In a large, heavy skillet over medium-low heat, heat a thin layer of olive oil until hot but not smoking. Fry the fritters in 2 batches until pale golden brown on both sides. Using a slotted metal spatula, transfer to paper towels to drain.

Pile the fritters on a platter and sprinkle with sumac or paprika. Serve hot, warm, or at room temperature, with lemon wedges.

SAVORY HONEY-PEAR PIES

If you like the combination of sweet and savory flavors, you'll enjoy these unusual little pies. The pastry is made with garbanzo bean flour, which gives it a nutty texture, and the pear filling is sweetened with honey and sharpened with red wine vinegar. Perfect with a creamy young feta cheese or slices of aged graviera or Italian pecorino cheese and Watercress with Piquant Currant Sauce (page 63).

Makes 8 half-moon pies; 8 meze or 4 side-dish servings

FILLING

1 tablespoon red wine vinegar

2 tablespoons mild honey

2 firm, ripe pears, peeled, cored, and cut into ¼-inch dice

4 bay leaves

PASTRY

1½ cups unbleached all-purpose flour

½ cup garbanzo bean flour or whole-wheat flour

1 teaspoon sea salt

1 egg white

2 to 3 tablespoons extra-virgin olive oil, plus more for brushing

2 tablespoons fresh lemon juice

5 tablespoons water

¼ cup shelled walnuts, chopped

½ tablespoon dried thyme or winter savory, crumbled

Large pinch of fine salt

1 egg yolk

½ tablespoon red wine vinegar

½ tablespoon mild honey

3 tablespoons extra-virgin olive oil

TO MAKE THE FILLING: In a medium bowl, combine the vinegar and honey. Add the pears and bay leaves and carefully stir to mix. Cover and set aside for at least 4 hours or overnight.

TO MAKE THE PASTRY: Sift the all-purpose flour, and garbanzo bean or whole-wheat flour and salt into a large bowl. In a medium bowl, whisk the egg white until soft peaks form. Stir into the flour with 2 tablespoons of the olive oil, the lemon juice, and 2 tablespoons of the water. On a lightly floured board, knead for 5 to 10 minutes, adding up to 1 tablespoon more olive oil as needed to make an elastic dough. Be patient; for the first few minutes of kneading, the dough will appear dry. Tightly wrap in plastic wrap and refrigerate for 1 hour. Remove the filling from the refrigerator 1 hour before you make the pies.

Preheat the oven to 350°F. Brush a heavy baking sheet with

olive oil. Pour off any juice from the filling and reserve it; discard the bay leaves. Add the walnuts, thyme or savory, fine salt, and enough of the reserved juice to moisten the pears (but don't make too wet, or your pastry will harden in baking). Gently mix with a wooden spoon.

TO MAKE THE PIES: Remove the dough from the refrigerator and divide in half. Rewrap one portion and refrigerate it. Roll the dough out as thin as possible. Cut into four 4-inch circles with a cookie cutter or an inverted glass. Place 1 heaped tablespoon filling in the center of each. Dip your forefinger in 2 tablespoons of the water and lightly dampen the pastry edges. Fold the circles over to make half-moons. Seal by gently pressing the edges together with a pastry wheel or the prongs of a fork. Place the pies 1 inch apart on the prepared pan and repeat with the remaining pastry and filling. Liberally brush the pies with the olive oil and bake for 10 minutes, or until set. Whisk the remaining 1 tablespoon water into the egg yolk and brush the pastries with this glaze. Bake for 10 to 15 minutes, or until golden brown.

Meanwhile, combine the vinegar, honey, the 3 tablespoons olive oil, and any remaining juice from the filling; pour into a small serving bowl. Serve the pies hot, warm, or at room temperature, with the sauce alongside.

VARIATION: The filling is also good in small or tiny pies made with yogurt pastry (page 102) or in filo pies (page 101).

OLIVE CIGAR PIES

Named for their shape, and with a texture between bread and pastry, these herb-and-coriander-scented pies are country classics. The dough is made with olive oil, and the filling is either mixed into the dough to make a rustic bread or bread "cigars," or placed in the center of the pastry as a culinary surprise.

If using mild, sweet Amfissa olives or light, brine-cured olives, serve with Little Cheeses in Olive Oil (page 19) or salads; if using the powerful Thasos olives or other salt-cured olives, serve with preserved fish or meats, grills, or rich vegetable or fish soups.

Makes 8 pies or 2 small loaves; 8 meze or 4 side-dish servings

PASTRY

½ teaspoon honey

¼ warm (105° to 115°F) water, plus 1 tablespoon

1 package (2½ teaspoons) active dried yeast

1½ cups unbleached white bread flour, plus more as needed

½ teaspoon fine sea salt

1 egg

¼ cup extra-virgin olive oil

FILLING

2 tablespoons extra-virgin olive oil

1 onion, finely chopped

12 Amfissa or light, brine-cured fleshy olives, or Thasos or salt-cured black olives

½ teaspoon ground coriander

¼ cup minced fresh flat-leaf parsley, fennel, cilantro, or watercress, or a mixture

1 tablespoon dried Greek oregano or rigani, crumbled

1 tablespoon fresh lemon juice

Freshly ground pepper to taste

½ cup small-curd cottage cheese or ricotta cheese, drained for 15 minutes

Extra-virgin olive oil for brushing

TO MAKE THE PASTRY: In a small bowl, mix the honey and ¼ cup lukewarm water together. Sprinkle the yeast over. Set aside in a warm place for 10 minutes, or until foamy.

Sift 1½ cups of the flour and the salt into a medium bowl and make a well in the center. In a small bowl, beat the egg and the 1 tablespoon water together, then whisk in the olive oil and the yeast mixture; pour into the flour and stir to blend. Turn out onto a lightly floured board and knead for 10 to 15 minutes, adding the remaining flour, 1 tablespoon at a time as necessary, to make a firm but elastic dough. Place in an oiled bowl, turn to coat, and cover the bowl with plastic wrap or a damp kitchen towel. Set aside in a warm place until doubled in bulk, about 1 hour.

TO MAKE THE FILLING: In a medium, heavy skillet over low heat, heat the olive oil and cook the onion for about 10 minutes, or until soft and just beginning to color. Blanch the olives in boiling water for 30 seconds. Drain, pit, and finely chop. Add the ground coriander to the skillet and heat until fragrant. Add the olives, parsley or other herb, and oregano, and cook for 1 minute. Sprinkle with lemon juice and pepper, stir to mix, and set aside. When cold, lightly stir in the cheese.

TO MAKE 8 SMALL PIES: Divide the dough into 8 portions and place 1 portion on a lightly floured board. Flatten with the palm of your hand, then roll out to make a 4-inch circle. Place one-eighth of the filling in the center. Fold over the two opposite sides to overlap, leaving some filling exposed at each end. Lightly press down with the palm of your hand to slightly flatten the pie. Repeat with the remaining dough and filling.

TO MAKE BREAD ROLLS OR 2 SMALL LOAVES: Add the olive mixture to the dough and knead for 1 minute; don't worry if the dough appears to collapse, as it will revive after resting. For rolls, divide into 8 portions; roll 1 portion between your palms to make a cigar shape with tapered ends; repeat with the remaining dough. To make 2 loaves, divide the dough into 2 portions and flatten each one with the palm of your hand.

Brush a heavy baking sheet with olive oil and arrange the pies, rolls, or loaves on it, spaced at least 3 inches apart. Let rise for 1 hour in a warm place.

Preheat the oven to 375°F. Brush the pies or bread with the olive oil and bake for 5 minutes. Reduce the oven temperature to 350°F and bake small pies or rolls for 15 minutes or loaves for 25 minutes, or until golden brown.

Transfer to wire racks to cool slightly or completely, and serve warm or at room temperature.

PEPPERED GREEK OREGANO PORK

The meat in this dish is cut into thin strips, refrigerated for at least an hour in a peppery garlic-and-bay-scented marinade, then quickly sautéed. After that, all it needs is a sprinkling of aromatic Greek oregano (rigani) and a judicious dash of lemon juice to lend just the right astringency. Shredded cabbage, lightly cooked in the pan juices, provides the perfect complement. Serve with black olives, feta cheese, country bread, and a glass of ouzo or tsipouro for a tasty, informal supper.

Makes 8 meze or 2 main-course servings

12 ounces pork tenderloin, cut into ¼-inch-thick diagonal strips

1 teaspoon finely cracked pepper

7 tablespoons extra-virgin olive oil

8 bay leaves, broken into large pieces

2 cloves garlic

1 tablespoon dried Greek oregano or rigani, crumbled

Juice of 1 small lemon

Coarse sea salt to taste

3 cups shredded cabbage

Put the meat in a bowl. Sprinkle with the pepper, 2 tablespoons of the olive oil, and the bay leaves. Crush the garlic cloves with the side of a heavy knife and add to the bowl. Cover and refrigerate for 1 hour.

In a heavy skillet over low to medium-low heat, heat 1 tablespoon of the olive oil. Add the pork, bay leaves, and marinade; discard the garlic. Sauté the meat for about 6 minutes, or until browned on all sides. Sprinkle with the oregano. Reduce heat to low and add the lemon juice. Stir to scrape up the browned bits from the bottom of the pan. Simmer for a minute or two, then stir in 2 tablespoons of the olive oil. Spoon everything onto one side of a warmed platter. Sprinkle with salt and keep warm.

Return the skillet to low heat and add the remaining 2 tablespoons olive oil. Add the cabbage and stir to scrape up all the pan juices and any remaining browned bits. Increase heat to medium-low and continue cooking and stirring for 1 minute, or until the cabbage softens. Transfer to the platter and arrange alongside the meat. Sprinkle with salt and serve immediately.

FETA & LAMB PIES

Although filo pies look intricate, they are not difficult to make. In this version, the filling is ground lamb seasoned with allspice, Greek oregano, and pepper and topped with a feta and curd cheese mixture.

Makes 12 small or 16 tiny pies; 8 or 12 meze or 4 light main-course servings

3   tablespoons extra-virgin olive oil, plus more for brushing

6   ounces lean lamb, finely ground

1   small onion, grated

1   teaspoon ground allspice

2   tomatoes, peeled, seeded, and diced (see page 126); juices reserved

2   tablespoons minced fresh flat-leaf parsley

1   tablespoon dried Greek oregano or rigani, crumbled

Sea salt and freshly ground pepper to taste

2/3 cup (4 ounces) feta cheese, grated

1/4 cup small-curd cottage cheese, drained for 15 minutes

4   fresh or thawed frozen filo pastry sheets

In a heavy skillet over low heat, heat 2 tablespoons of the olive oil and cook the meat, stirring occasionally, for about 10 minutes, or until evenly browned. Using a slotted spoon, transfer to paper towels to drain. Return the skillet to low heat and add 1 tablespoon of the olive oil. Sauté the onion until soft, about 5 minutes. Return the meat to the skillet. Add the allspice, tomatoes and their juice, parsley, oregano, salt, and pepper. Simmer until thickened. Taste and adjust the seasoning (the filling should be highly flavored). Set aside to cool. Combine the feta cheese and cottage cheese. Season with pepper.

Preheat the oven to 350°F. Brush a heavy baking sheet with olive oil. Stack the filo pastry sheets on a work surface with a shorter side facing you. Cut the sheets lengthwise into 3 strips (for small pies) or 4 strips (for tiny pies). Stack the strips on top of each other. Carefully remove the top strip from the pile and lightly brush with olive oil.

To make small pies, place 1 heaped tablespoon meat filling on the bottom end of the oiled strip and 1 scant tablespoon of cheese filling on top of the meat. For tiny pies, use 1 scant tablespoon meat filling and 1 teaspoon cheese filling. To make triangles, take the bottom right-hand corner of the strip and fold over to the left side; take care to keep the filling in place. Gently pull up the bottom left corner and fold over to make a second triangle. Continue folding until you reach the top. To make rolls, fold the lower edge of the strip over the filling and roll over twice, then bring both sides over the filling and roll up the strip.

Place seam-side down on the prepared pan and repeat with the remaining filo and filling. Arrange the pies 1 inch apart on the baking sheet and brush with olive oil. Bake for 15 to 20 minutes, or until golden brown. Serve warm.

❧❧❧❧❧❧

VARIATION: For crisper pies, use 2 layers of filo for each pie; brush the first pastry strip with olive oil before you lay the second strip on top (you will need 8 filo sheets instead of 4).

❧❧❧❧❧❧

TINY VEGETABLE PIES

The filling for these pies is one of my favorites: red bell peppers, eggplant, and crunchy pine nuts animated with allspice and coriander, thyme or marjoram, and parsley. The vegetables can be varied according to season, and leftover vegetables, especially roasted ones, work well too. Serve warm or at room temperature with a salad, cheese, and olives, or hot with grilled meats.

Makes 8 small or 12 tiny pies; 8 meze or 4 side-dish servings

YOGURT PASTRY

2 cups unbleached all-purpose flour

1 teaspoon sea salt

½ teaspoon superfine sugar

1 egg white

2 to 3 tablespoons extra-virgin olive oil

⅓ cup Village Yogurt (page 17)

FILLING

Small handful of young beet greens or spinach, stemmed

5 tablespoons extra-virgin olive oil

1 eggplant, cut into ½-inch dice, or 1 large zucchini, cut into ¼-inch dice

1 leek, white part only, cut into very thin slices and rinsed, or 1 onion, finely chopped

1 red bell pepper, roasted, peeled, and cut into short slivers (see page 123)

¼ teaspoon ground allspice

½ teaspoon ground coriander

1 tablespoon dried thyme or marjoram, crumbled

¼ cup minced fresh flat-leaf parsley

¼ cup pine nuts, toasted and chopped (see page 124)

1 tablespoon fresh lemon juice

1 teaspoon sea salt, or to taste

½ teaspoon freshly ground pepper, or to taste

2 tablespoons extra-virgin olive oil for brushing

3 tablespoons water

1 egg yolk

TO MAKE THE PASTRY: Sift the flour, salt, and sugar into a large bowl. In a medium bowl, whisk the egg white until soft peaks form. Stir into the flour with 2 tablespoons of the olive oil and the yogurt. On a lightly floured board, knead for 5 to 10 minutes, adding up to 1 tablespoon more olive oil as needed to make an elastic dough. Be patient; for the first few minutes of kneading, the dough will appear dry. Tightly wrap in plastic wrap and refrigerate for 1 hour.

TO MAKE THE FILLING: Add the greens to a large, heavy saucepan. Cover and cook over low heat for about 2 minutes, or until wilted, stirring once or twice. Drain and squeeze dry with paper towels. Coarsely chop the greens. In a heavy skillet over low heat, heat 3 tablespoons of the olive oil and sauté the eggplant for about 12 minutes, or until browned on all sides; cook zucchini for about 8 minutes, or until just starting to color. Using a slotted spoon, transfer to paper towels to drain. Add the remaining 2 tablespoons olive oil to the skillet and sauté the leek until soft, about 4 minutes. Add the greens and the remaining filling ingredients, then add the eggplant. Gently stir to mix, and heat through. Taste and adjust the seasoning (the filling should be highly flavored). Set aside.

Preheat the oven to 375°F. Brush a heavy baking sheet with olive oil. Remove the dough from the refrigerator and divide in half. Rewrap one portion and refrigerate it. Roll the dough out as thin as possible.

TO MAKE 8 HALF MOON PIES: Cut into four 4-inch circles with a cookie cutter or inverted glass. Place 1 heaped tablespoon filling in the center of each. Dip your forefinger in 2 tablespoons water and lightly dampen the pastry edges. Fold the circles over to make half-moons. Seal by gently pressing the edges together with a pastry wheel or the prongs of a fork. To make 8 small, or 16 tiny, square pies with filling enclosed: Cut the pastry into four 2-by-4-inch or eight 1½-by-3-inch rectangles. Place one-eighth (or one-sixteenth) of the filling in the center of one half of each rectangle. Dip your finger in 2 tablespoons water and run it along the pastry edges to lightly dampen. Fold over to make squares, and seal by crimping the edges with a pastry wheel or fork. Repeat with the remaining pastry and filling.

Place the pies 1 inch apart on the prepared pan and brush with the olive oil. Bake for 10 minutes, or until the pastry is set. Whisk 1 tablespoon water into the egg yolk and brush the pastries with this glaze. Bake for 10 to 15 minutes, or until golden brown. Serve hot, warm, or at room temperature.

VARIATION: For a quicker dish, use 8 filo pastry sheets. Stack the filo pastry sheets on a work surface with a shorter side facing you. Cut the sheets lengthwise into 3 strips. Stack the strips on top of each other. Carefully remove the top strip from the pile, lightly brush with olive oil, and lay a second strip on top. Place one-eighth of the filling on the bottom end of the oiled strip. To make triangles, take the bottom right-hand corner of the strip and fold over to the left side; take care to keep the filling in place. Gently pull up the bottom left corner and fold over to make a second triangle. Continue folding until you reach the top. To make rolls, fold the lower edge of the strip over the filling and roll over twice, then bring both sides over the filling, and roll up the strip. Place seam-side down on the prepared pan and repeat with the remaining filo and filling. Arrange the pies 1 inch apart on the baking sheet and brush with olive oil. Bake for 15 to 20 minutes, or until golden brown.

FROM THE GRILL

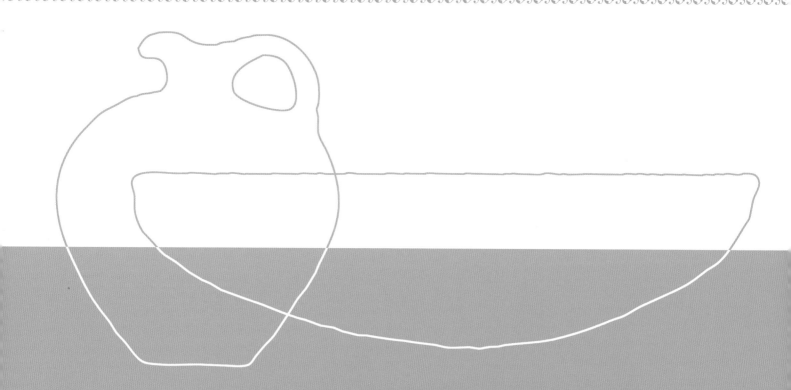

Summer is synonymous with outdoor cooking, and Greek grilled foods have a robust intensity of flavor that makes them perfect for this time of year. The country scents, the aromatic sizzle, and the smell of smoke evoke the atmosphere of Greek villages on long summer evenings. While the fire heats up, villagers exchange gossip over a glass of wine or ouzo, nibbling on smoky eggplant and sweet pepper appetizers, the first of the evening's offerings from the grill.

Later, taste buds are tingled and hunger satisfied by moist patties (*kephtedes*) of meat or fish, pungent with hillside herbs and garlic, and spicy skewers (*souvlakia*) of tender lean meat or firm-fleshed fish. Lamb is the meat of choice for grilling, either marinated cubes threaded on skewers, or a succulent piece of lamb on the bone. But other traditional favorites are souvlakia made with chicken, pork, or fish; pieces of tender grilled rabbit; meze sausages; or fish or vegetable patties.

Mezes from the spit and grill burst with smoky flavor. This is balmy-weather food, great to eat in the garden or on the deck while chatting with friends. If you don't have a grill, cook your souvlakia or kephtedes under the broiler or in an oiled hot grill pan.

SALT-GRILLED PRAWNS WITH HONEY-VINEGAR SAUCE

This simple summer dish has a timeless appeal. Dipping prawns into olive oil and vinegar and sprinkling them with sea salt before grilling highlights the natural subtlety of their flavor and gives them a crisp crust. The bitter and crunchy frisée and green onion salad with a mustard dressing is the perfect partner. Serve with olives and Meze Breads (page 30).

Makes 8 meze or 4 first-course servings

8 jumbo or 16 large fresh prawns in the shell, preferably with heads intact

1½ tablespoons red wine vinegar

6 tablespoons extra-virgin olive oil, plus more for brushing

2 small branches fresh or dried rosemary, or 3 large bay leaves, tied together to make a basting brush (optional)

2 tablespoons coarse sea salt, plus salt to taste

¼ teaspoon Meaux mustard or other good-quality mild whole-grain mustard

½ tablespoon Hymettus or other strongly flavored honey

Tender inner leaves from 1 small frisée lettuce, torn into pieces

2 green onions, including the unblemished green parts, cut into diagonal slivers

Freshly ground pepper to taste

Prepare a fire in a charcoal grill. With a small, sharp knife, carefully cut into each prawn shell along the back. Pull out and discard the black vein. Thoroughly rinse the prawns under cold running water and pat dry with paper towels.

In a shallow bowl, whisk together 1 tablespoon of the vinegar and 4 tablespoons of the olive oil. Dip each prawn into this sauce. Brush the grill grids or a grill basket with olive oil, using the herb brush, if desired. Place the prawns on the grill or in the basket and sprinkle with 1 tablespoon of the salt. Grill for 5 minutes, or just until pink, brushing once with the sauce (disturb the salt as little as possible). Turn the prawns, sprinkle with the remaining 1 tablespoon salt, and grill, brushing once with the sauce, for 4 minutes, or until lightly scorched and crusty.

Meanwhile, in a medium bowl, combine the mustard, honey, and remaining ½ tablespoon vinegar. Whisk in the remaining 2 tablespoons olive oil. Add the frisée and green onions. Lightly toss all together and season with salt and pepper to taste.

To serve, spread the frisée salad over a platter and arrange the prawns on top. Serve any remaining sauce alongside.

VARIATION: To add fragrance to the prawns, sprinkle grapevine clippings or sprigs of woody herbs such as rosemary or sage over the coals just before grilling.

SARDINES IN A PARCEL

Grilled fresh sardines need little embellishment, but this Greek method of wrapping them in grape leaves and grilling them quickly adds a pungent leaf flavor. Small pieces of bonito or tuna are also delicious prepared this way.

A lemony sauce cuts through the oiliness of the sardines, and a garnish of radishes, green onion, and olives adds color. The starchiness of the mashed garbanzo beans is an ideal foil for the fish. Sardines cook in minutes, so have the rest of your meze table ready before you begin grilling.

Makes 8 meze or first-course servings,
4 light main-course servings

½ cup dried garbanzo beans

8 plump fresh sardines, heads and tails discarded, or 1¼ pounds tuna or bonito fillets, cut into eight ½-inch-thick pieces

Juice of 1 lemon

Coarse sea salt and freshly ground pepper to taste

16 fresh grape leaves, stemmed

Extra-virgin olive oil for brushing, plus 7 tablespoons

¼ teaspoon paprika

Large pinch of ground coriander

¼ teaspoon Dijon mustard

1 tablespoon snipped fresh chives

1 tablespoon minced fresh flat-leaf parsley

8 radishes, base leaves intact

8 slender green onions, including unblemished green parts

16 Elitses or niçoise olives

Rinse and pick over the beans. Soak overnight in cold water to cover by 2 inches. Drain the beans, rinse well, and put in a saucepan with cold water to cover by 3 inches. Bring to a boil, reduce heat to low, cover, and simmer for about 40 minutes, or until tender; drain and set aside.

Prepare a fire in a charcoal grill. Rub the sardines or fillets with a little of the lemon juice, the salt, and pepper. Brush both sides of the grape leaves with olive oil and, using 2 leaves for each sardine, wrap up each one to make a packet. Secure with a toothpick.

Put the garbanzo beans in a mortar or bowl and sprinkle with salt and pepper to taste, 2 tablespoons of the olive oil, and ½ tablespoon of the lemon juice. With a pestle or wooden spoon, mash to a coarse paste. Arrange on one side of a serving platter and sprinkle with the paprika.

Brush the grill grids or a grill basket with olive oil. Grill the sardines for 2 to 3 minutes on each side, turning once; cook tuna or bonito for 2 to 3 minutes, or until just slightly translucent in the center.

Meanwhile, put the remaining lemon juice, the coriander, mustard, chives, parsley, and salt and pepper to taste in a serving bowl. Whisk in the remaining 5 tablespoons olive oil. Place the bowl on the platter alongside the mashed garbanzo beans and surround with the sardine packets; remove the toothpicks. Garnish with radishes, green onions, and olives, and serve at once. (The grape leaves are not eaten.)

THYME-SCENTED FISH SOUVLAKIA WITH ROASTED-PEPPER SAUCE

Firm-fleshed fish such as porgy or swordfish make flavorsome souvlakia. They are very easy to prepare, but keep a careful eye on the grilling to make sure the fish is not overcooked.

Porgy and swordfish have distinctive flavors, so accompanying sauces need depth and character. This classic sauce of bell peppers with a hint of anchovy and garlic is just right. It can be used warm or cold, and it's also good for lightly cooked vegetables and leftover chicken and pork. Serve with Kos Lentils & Olives (page 70), country bread, and a glass of crisp white wine.

Makes 8 meze or 4 light main-course servings

24 one-inch squares firm, white fish such as porgy or swordfish (about 1¼ pounds total)

Juice of ½ a lemon

Coarse sea salt and freshly ground pepper to taste

8 tablespoons extra-virgin olive oil

2 shallots, minced

1 clove garlic, minced

1 salt-packed anchovy fillet, rinsed, soaked, patted dry, and chopped (see page 118)

Large pinch of ground allspice

1 red bell pepper, roasted, peeled, and chopped (see page 123)

1 teaspoon red wine vinegar

¼ cup coarsely chopped fresh flat-leaf parsley

2 small branches thyme or 3 large bay leaves, tied together to make a basting brush (optional)

1½ tablespoons chopped fresh thyme, or 1 tablespoon dried thyme, crumbled

Light a fire in a charcoal grill. Sprinkle the fish with half the lemon juice, the salt, and pepper. Set aside for 30 minutes. Soak 4 to 8 small wooden skewers in water for 30 minutes.

Meanwhile, make the sauce: In a small, heavy saucepan over low heat, heat 3 tablespoons of the olive oil and cook the shallots for about 4 minutes, or until soft. Add the garlic and cook for 1 minute, or until fragrant. Stir in the anchovy and allspice. Transfer to a food processor or mortar. Add the bell pepper, salt and pepper to taste, and the vinegar. Process or pound with a pestle until smooth. Add the parsley and 2 tablespoons of the olive oil and process or pound until blended. Taste and adjust the seasoning.

Drain the skewers and thread 3 fish pieces onto each of 8 skewers or 6 pieces onto 4 skewers. Gently push the pieces together. Whisk the remaining 3 tablespoons olive oil and the remaining lemon juice together and liberally brush the souvlakia with this sauce. Grill the souvlakia for about 4 minutes, or until opaque throughout, turning once and basting frequently with the herb brush, if using. Add the thyme to the sauce for the final baste.

To serve, spread the bell pepper sauce over a warmed platter and arrange the souvlakia on top. Sprinkle with salt and pepper to taste, and any remaining basting sauce.

MARINATED KALAMARIA WITH WALNUT-GARLIC SAUCE

The unusual sauce for this dish of grilled squid dates from the kitchens of antiquity, and it's still as popular today. With a food processor you can make it in a flash, but you'll produce a thicker, more intensely flavored sauce by pounding the ingredients in a mortar. The sauce also marries well with other fried fish and with bean dishes, steamed or baked zucchini, or fried eggplant. Serve with olives and a green salad.

Makes 8 meze or 4 first-course servings

8 small squid (1¼ pounds), cleaned (see page 126)

2 tablespoons fresh lemon juice

1 tablespoon Hymettus or other strongly flavored honey

Coarse sea salt and freshly ground pepper to taste

2 tablespoons extra-virgin olive oil, plus more for brushing

WALNUT-GARLIC SAUCE

½ cup walnuts

1 to 2 plump cloves garlic (to taste), minced

Coarse sea salt and freshly ground pepper to taste

¼ cup coarse fresh bread crumbs, lightly toasted (see page 118)

¼ cup minced fresh flat-leaf parsley or cilantro

2 tablespoons extra-virgin olive oil

½ tablespoon fresh lemon juice

2 tablespoons broth, milk, or extra-virgin olive oil

Cucumber slices and lemon wedges for garnish

Cut the squid bodies in half and open flat. Rinse well and spread on paper towels to dry. In a medium bowl, mix the lemon juice, honey, salt, pepper, and the 2 tablespoons olive oil together. Add the squid and stir to coat with the marinade. Cover and set aside for 1 hour.

Meanwhile, light a fire in a charcoal grill and make the sauce: In a food processor or mortar, process or pound the nuts and garlic until pulverized and somewhat oily, about 1 minute in a processor, 6 minutes in a mortar. Add the salt, pepper, bread crumbs, and parsley or cilantro and process or pound to mix. Gradually add the olive oil, lemon juice, and the broth, milk, or olive oil. Taste and adjust the seasoning. Set aside.

Remove the squid from the marinade. Brush 4 medium metal skewers with olive oil. Thread each piece of squid lengthwise onto the skewers and spear the tentacles, too. Liberally brush the grill grids with olive oil and the squid with marinade. Grill the squid for 1 to 2 minutes on each side, or until lightly charred outside and opaque throughout. With a fork, push the squid off the skewers onto a warmed platter. Heap the walnut sauce alongside. Garnish with cucumber slices and lemon wedges.
Serve warm.

TAVERNA LAMB

The traditional Greek alliance of lamb and lemon is an inspired partnership. Here, the lamb takes its citrus accent from a lemon marinade, later used as a basting sauce. The souvlakia are served on a bed of romaine lettuce and parsley, with wafer-thin rings of red onion and plenty of lemon wedges. As a main course, serve with Village Yogurt (page 17), olives, and Meze Breads (page 30).

Makes 8 meze or 4 light main-course servings

1 pound lean leg of lamb, trimmed and cut into 1-inch or 1½-inch cubes

Juice of 1 lemon (reserve 1 juiced lemon half for basting)

Freshly ground pepper to taste

6 tablespoons extra-virgin olive oil

1 red onion, quartered and cut into very thin slices

1 teaspoon sumac, or ½ teaspoon paprika

½ cup coarsely chopped fresh flat-leaf parsley

Tender inner leaves from 1 small romaine lettuce, thinly sliced (about 2 cups)

1 tablespoon dried Greek oregano or rigani, crumbled

Coarse sea salt to taste

Lemon wedges for garnish

In a medium bowl, combine the lamb, half of the lemon juice, the pepper, and 4 tablespoons of the olive oil. Stir to coat the lamb. Cover and set aside for 2 hours.

Prepare a fire in a charcoal grill. Soak 8 short or 4 long wooden skewers in water for 30 minutes. Drain the skewers and the lamb, reserving the marinade. Thread the smaller pieces of lamb onto the 8 short skewers, or the larger pieces onto the 4 longer skewers. Secure the half-lemon on the tip of a spare skewer and dip in the marinade; use it to baste both grill grids and meat. Grill the souvlakia, turning once and liberally and frequently basting with the marinade, for 8 to 10 minutes, or until browned on both sides.

Meanwhile, combine the onion, sumac or paprika, remaining lemon juice, pepper to taste, and parsley in a large bowl. Add the lettuce, sprinkle with the remaining 2 tablespoons olive oil, and lightly toss to coat.

To serve, spread the salad over a platter and arrange the souvlakia on top. Or, with a fork, push the souvlakia from each skewer onto the salad. Sprinkle with oregano and salt, and surround with lemon wedges.

SAGE-GRILLED CHICKEN
SOUVLAKIA & OLIVES

Before cooking, the chicken pieces are marinated in a mustard, sage, honey, and olive oil paste, resulting in tender chicken packed with intriguing flavor. The chicken is served on a cushion of bread crumbs gently sautéed with shallots, pine nuts, sage, and chives.

Makes 8 meze or 4 light main-course servings

2 skinless, boneless chicken breast halves, cut into 16 or 24 pieces

½ cup packed fresh sage leaves

Juice of ½ a lemon

½ tablespoon Hymettus or other strongly flavored honey

1 teaspoon Meaux mustard or other good-quality mild whole-grain mustard

Freshly ground pepper to taste

½ teaspoon ground bay leaf

9 tablespoons extra-virgin olive oil

16 kalamata olives, pitted

4 shallots, minced

½ cup pine nuts, lightly toasted (see page 124)

2 cups coarse fresh whole-wheat bread crumbs, lightly toasted (see page 118)

¼ cup snipped fresh chives

Coarse sea salt to taste

Sage sprigs and lemon wedges for garnish

In a medium bowl, combine the chicken and 6 of the sage leaves. Sprinkle with half the lemon juice. Combine the honey, mustard, pepper, bay leaf, remaining lemon juice, and 2 tablespoons of the olive oil. Pour over the chicken and stir to coat each piece. Cover and set aside for 1 hour. Flatten each olive with the side of a heavy knife and put in a bowl. Stir in 1 tablespoon of the olive oil and set aside for 1 hour.

Prepare a charcoal grill. Soak 16 small wooden skewers in water for 30 minutes. Prepare the bread crumbs: Stack 4 or 5 of the sage leaves and cut into thin ribbons; repeat with the remaining leaves. In a heavy skillet over low heat, heat 2 tablespoons of the olive oil and cook the shallots for about 4 minutes, or until soft. Add another 2 tablespoons of the olive oil, the pine nuts, bread crumbs, and sage leaf ribbons. Sauté, stirring occasionally, for about 4 minutes, or until the bread crumbs are golden and the sage is fragrant. Stir in the chives and season with salt and pepper; set aside and keep warm.

Drain the skewers. Thread 2 to 3 chicken pieces on each of 8 skewers and brush with the remaining 2 tablespoons olive oil and any remaining marinade; discard the sage leaves. Thread 2 olives lengthwise onto each of the remaining 8 skewers. Brush the grill or a grill basket with olive oil and grill the chicken for 2 minutes. Place the olives on the grill or in the grill basket. Grill, turning both chicken and olives once, for 4 or 5 minutes, or until the chicken is golden brown and the olives are crinkled. Sprinkle the chicken with salt to taste and remove from the grill.

Spread the bread crumb mixture over a warmed platter and arrange the souvlakia on top. Garnish with sage sprigs and lemon wedges. Serve immediately.

LEAF-WRAPPED KEPHTEDES WITH YOGURT SAUCE

These dainty mouthfuls, which appeal to all ages and tastes, always disappear very quickly at parties. Everyone seems to like the scented flavor and moist texture that come from cooking the patty mixture in a leaf wrap. Make these one day ahead for the flavor to develop a spicy intensity.

Makes 8 meze or 4 first-course servings

¼ cup fine-grain bulgur wheat

6 tablespoons lukewarm water

1 small onion, finely chopped

¼ cup plus 2 tablespoons cold water

12 ounces lean lamb, finely ground

1 egg, well beaten

1 teaspoon sea salt

½ teaspoon freshly ground pepper

½ teaspoon ground coriander

2 tablespoons minced fresh flat-leaf parsley

1 tablespoon dried Greek oregano or rigani, crumbled

16 fresh or preserved grape leaves, 4 to 5 inches across at the widest point, blanched or soaked (see page 120)

3 tablespoons extra-virgin olive oil, plus more for brushing

Juice of ½ a small lemon

YOGURT SAUCE

1 small clove garlic, minced, or to taste

Sea salt to taste

1 tablespoon extra-virgin olive oil

1 cup Village Yogurt (page 17)

Freshly ground pepper to taste

1 tablespoon minced fresh flat-leaf parsley

1 tablespoon dried Greek oregano or rigani, crumbled

¼ teaspoon sumac or large pinch of paprika

Lemon wedges for garnish

In a large bowl, combine the bulgur and lukewarm water. Cover and set aside for 15 minutes.

In a small saucepan, combine the onion and the ¼ cup water. Bring to a simmer over very low heat and cook for about 6 minutes, or until almost dry.

Add the lamb, onion, egg, salt, pepper, coriander, parsley, and oregano to the bulgur. Knead with your hand or a wooden spoon until well mixed; continue kneading for 1 minute. Cover and refrigerate for at least 30 minutes or, preferably, overnight.

(continued on page 116)

Light a fire in a charcoal grill. Form the meat mixture into eight 2-inch-long barrel shapes. Put 2 grape leaves on your palm, glossy-side down and overlapping, and arrange 1 meat barrel in the center. Fold in the sides of the grape leaves and carefully roll up to make a packet with the filling completely enclosed; secure with a toothpick. Lay the packets side by side on a cutting board and place a second board on top. With the palm of your hand, carefully press the top board to evenly flatten the packets to about ½ inch thick; set aside for at least 15 minutes or up to 30 minutes. To store longer, place the packets in a shallow dish and cover with plastic wrap. Refrigerate no longer than 4 hours and bring to room temperature before grilling.

In a small bowl, whisk 3 tablespoons of the olive oil, the lemon juice, and the 2 tablespoons water together. Brush the grill grids or a grill basket with olive oil and grill the packets on both sides for about 8 minutes, or until cooked but still moist inside; baste frequently with the sauce.

Meanwhile, make the yogurt sauce: In a bowl, combine the garlic and salt; pound to a paste with a pestle or wooden spoon. Stir in the olive oil, yogurt, pepper, parsley, and oregano. Transfer to a serving bowl and sprinkle with the sumac or paprika.

Arrange the packets on a warm platter and remove the toothpicks. Surround with lemon wedges and serve the yogurt sauce alongside.

SPICY LAMB KEPHTEDES WITH ARUGULA & GRILLED LEMON

Succulent grilled patties on a bed of greens, garnished with shiny lemon wedges, are one of Greece's simplest, most satisfying pleasures. Be generous with herbs and spices in the patty mixture; the flavor should be bold. Keep a close eye on timing and heat when grilling kephtedes to make sure they stay moist inside. Frequent basting with olive oil helps, and using herb sprigs as a basting brush, as village cooks do, produces beautifully fragrant patties.

Makes 8 meze or 4 light main-course servings

1 small onion, finely chopped

¼ cup water

1 small clove garlic, minced

2 teaspoons cumin seeds, toasted and ground (see page 125)

½ teaspoon sea salt, plus more to taste

12 ounces lean ground lamb

1 teaspoon dried Greek oregano or rigani, crumbled

¼ cup minced fresh flat-leaf parsley

¼ cup snipped fresh chives or finely chopped green onion leaves

1 tablespoon fresh lemon juice, plus 4 lemons, halved crosswise

¼ teaspoon freshly ground pepper, plus more to taste

2 small branches dried Greek oregano or rigani, or fresh or dried rosemary, marjoram, thyme, or bay leaves, tied together to make a basting brush (optional)

Extra-virgin olive oil for brushing, plus 2 tablespoons

Large handful of tender arugula, stemmed

In a small saucepan, combine the onion and water. Bring to a simmer over very low heat and cook for about 6 minutes, or until almost dry.

In a mortar or small bowl, combine the garlic, cumin, and salt. Pound with a pestle or wooden spoon until pulverized.

In a large bowl, combine the meat, onion, oregano, parsley, chives or green onion, lemon juice, and pepper. Add the garlic mixture. Knead with your hand for 5 minutes. Cover and refrigerate for at least 2 or up to 4 hours.

Prepare a fire in a charcoal grill. Wet your hands and shape the meat mixture into 8 balls. Slightly flatten each ball between your palms to make a patty. Liberally brush the grill grids or a grill basket with olive oil, using the herb brush, if desired. Place the lemon halves, cut-sides down, on the grill or in the basket along with the patties. Grill, turning once, for about 8 minutes, or until browned and crusty on the outside, but still moist inside; brush frequently with olive oil.

Just before the kephtedes are ready, place a broiler tray over the coals and pour in the 2 tablespoons olive oil. Add the arugula and stir for about 1 minute, just to soften; sprinkle with salt and pepper to taste.

Fork the arugula onto a warmed platter and arrange the patties on top. Cut the lemon halves in half and surround the patties. Serve immediately.

GLOSSARY

ALMONDS

Essential to the traditional meze table, almonds have been cultivated in Greece for centuries. Dishes of almonds are served in cafés and bars, and salted or honey-coated almonds are sold on every street corner. During the Orthodox religious fasts, protein-rich almonds replace meat and dairy products on the meze table.

ANCHOVIES

A traditional flavoring in Greek cooking, anchovies are often used in judicious amounts to add piquancy to a dish.

RINSING AND SOAKING ANCHOVIES

Buy salt-packed whole anchovies imported from Greece or Italy; before using, rinse under cold running water and gently rub each between your finger and thumb to remove the salt, skin, and fins. Soak for 15 to 30 minutes in cold water containing a few drops of vinegar, then pat dry with paper towels. Oil-packed anchovy fillets may be used, but they should be drained, then soaked for 2 or 3 minutes; pat dry.

AVGOTARACHO

This is the amber-red roe of the gray mullet, which is pressed, smoked, and preserved under beeswax. Only whole roes are preserved, and the best come from mullet caught in the lagoons of Messalonghi in western Greece; avgotaracho is a costly luxury. Its rich salt-fish flavor has been a meze treat for over three thousand years, although its appeal is now mainly confined to the older generation. It can occasionally be found in Greek or Turkish groceries; remove the beeswax with a small knife, cut the roe into paper-thin slices, and serve on small pieces of toasted whole-wheat bread.

BONITO

Bonito has an assertive flavor and firm texture that is quite similar to tuna. Fried bonito makes a tasty inexpensive meze, but more prized is brine-cured bonito (lakertha), which can be found in Greek and Middle Eastern stores.

BREAD CRUMBS

Make your own fresh bread crumbs by grinding whole-wheat bread (crusts removed) in a blender to make coarse crumbs.

TOASTING BREAD CRUMBS

Spread the crumbs in a jellyroll pan and toast in a preheated 350°F oven for 8 to 10 minutes, or until lightly toasted; stir once or twice during this time.

BROWN RICE FLAKES

These are plain, lightly toasted flakes of rice. Crushed, unsalted rice cakes are a good substitute; you can find both rice flakes and rice cakes in natural foods stores.

BULGUR WHEAT

This is cracked wheat. For meze dishes, use fine or medium-fine bulgur. You can buy it in Greek, Middle Eastern, and natural foods stores.

CANDIES

Candied fruits were first exported to Europe during the Venetian occupation of Crete, which began in the thirteenth century and lasted four hundred years. The Venetians named the island Candia, from which we derive the word candy, and their merchants ran a profitable trade in Cretan honey, honey-coated fruits, and honey-sweet pastes. Fruit pastes and candied nuts are still popular sweet mezes.

CAPERS

Pickled capers are a central feature of the meze table. In spring, they are pickled with dill; in summer, the herb of choice is fennel fronds. The best are packed in coarse sea salt, and can be found in Greek, Italian, or specialty food stores. To use, soak them in cold water for 30 minutes, rinse under cold running water, and pat dry with paper towels. Brine-cured capers can be substituted, but some of their fine peppery flavor is lost; to use, drain, rinse well, and pat dry. Look, too, for caperberries and caper leaves, imported from Greece.

CHEESES

Greece produces few types of cheese, but each of those it does produce has a distinctive aroma and taste and many regional and seasonal variations. Greek cheeses owe their taste mainly to the flavor of the milk used: In winter and spring, when sheep and goats feed on grass, their milk has a soft, gentle flavor; in the long, dry summer, when pasture is scarce and the animals often graze on mountain herbs, the flavor is more pungent. In Greece, cheeses are named for their type, rather than their place of origin, and although there is now considerable commercial cheese production, there are also some wonderful artisanal cheeses and some very good traditional cheeses that are exported (see Resources). Here is a list of those you're most likely to find in the States, followed by a few to search for when you visit Greece.

IMPORTED CHEESES

FETA

The best feta, creamy white with a flaky texture and a fresh, mildly salty taste, is a blend of sheep's and goat's milk. Regional and seasonal variations differ slightly in taste and texture, although all versions have the characteristic salty flavor, due to being quickly ripened in a barrel of whey and brine. Ask for soft, medium, or hard feta, according to your recipe and taste, and look for feta from Epirus, or a Cephalonian version made with sheep's milk. If you bring the cheese home in some of the barrel's brine, it will keep a week or two in the refrigerator. You can find feta in Greek, natural foods, and specialty foods stores (or see Resources).

GRAVIERA

A slightly salted, full-flavored sheep's or cow's milk cheese with a thick rind. The best graviera is ripened for 3 to 6 months and develops a mellow, nutty flavor similar to Gruyère. Look for graviera ripened 6 months to 2 years, from Crete, in Greek or specialty foods stores (or see Resources). For a meze, serve this delicious cheese with walnuts, honey, and fresh figs.

KASSERI

A mild spun-curd cheese made from sheep's or cow's milk. Reliable and versatile, kasseri is a good table cheese; look for it in Greek or specialty foods stores.

KEPHALOTYRI

Named for its shape (like a head or hat), kephalotyri is a hard pale-yellow cheese made from either sheep's or goat's milk; the best is ripened for 2 to 4 months. Stored for 8 months, it has just the right hardness for *saganaki* (slices of cheese fried in olive oil and sprinkled with lemon juice), and cheeses over a year old are perfect for grating. Look for a semi-hard sheep's milk version from Crete, a good meze cheese that's perfect with fresh fruit. If you can't find kephalotyri, substitute Italian pecorino cheese.

KOPANISTI

Traditional kopanisti, named for the earthenware crocks in which it is ripened, is a pounded, semisoft sheep's milk blue cheese made exclusively on the islands. Sadly, the true island cheese is almost impossible to find, even in Greece, and the kopanisti on sale here is a "modern" version that substitutes flavorings, such as herbs or coriander seeds, for the crock-ripening process. Despite this, flavored kopanisti is a pleasant and unusual meze cheese; look for it in Greek stores.

MANOURI

A soft, white sheep's milk cheese with a rich, mild, creamy flavor, this is the best accompaniment to fresh or dried figs. Try it too with fresh fruit and honey, and a glass of sweet Samos wine. Look for manouri in Greek or specialty foods stores, or substitute a good-quality mozzarella.

MYZITHRA

During the fall, winter, and early spring, this soft, loose-textured white cheese is the centerpiece of many meze tables in Greece. Fresh myzithra is not available in the United States because of its short shelf life, but you can sometimes find aged myzithra, a pleasant grating cheese. A special myzithra, harder and with a deep yellow color, made near the Spartan town of Mystra, is said to be the origin of the cheese's name. Its lightly musty flavor is very good with nuts, dried figs, radishes, and mixed salad greens (see KHORTA).

LOCAL GREEK CHEESES

ANTHOTYRO

The name means "blossom cheese," and this exquisite, lightly salted fresh cheese is named for the way the curds "blossom" as they are stirred. If you visit Crete's Hania market in spring, be sure to try it.

FORMAELLA

A yellowish-white, sharp-flavored, semi-hard sheep cheese from Parnassus in central Greece, named after the basket mold *(forma)* in which it is traditionally made. Serve sliced, with pickles or capers. You will find this unusual cheese on specialty stands in Athens' central market.

LATHOTYRI

An island specialty, this hard pale-yellow sheep's cheese is traditionally molded in a small, tapering cylinder—a perfect shape for the meze table, a picnic, or a buffet. With a savory, slightly musty aroma and a pleasantly salty taste, it's delicious with black olives, nuts, and Meze Breads (page 30). Look for lathotyri from Zakynthos.

MEGITHRA

A flavored cheese from the Cyclades. The flavoring—usually Greek oregano, thyme, or ground coriander—is added to the curds at the first cutting. The curds are pressed into a goatskin bag and left to ripen for 4 months or more to produce a unique, slightly musty flavor. This is a cheese to seek out when you visit the Cyclades; try it with mezes of nuts, currants, and a small glass of the local sweet Santorini Visanto wine.

METSOVISSIO

A white, crumbly goat cheese, delicious with preserved meats and greens such as arugula, watercress, and purslane. Sometimes, the same name is given to a light, flaky goat cheese that is flavored with black peppercorns and is excellent with fresh or dried figs and bean dishes.

METSOVONE KAPNISTO

A cow's milk cheese smoked over vine cuttings and plane tree shavings, salted, hung a week or two, then preserved in wax. It's perfect with Amfissa olives, walnuts, and a green salad. This cheese, and the above one, are specialties of the Pindus mountain town of Metsovo.

CLAY POT COOKING

This cooking method, using no liquid or oil, produces a rich mellow flavor in baked foods, especially beets, potatoes, and mushrooms. Favored by the Minoan civilization on Crete three thousand years ago, it is still important in meze cooking. You can find unglazed clay pots in good kitchenware stores in the United States. The ideal pot has a wide base, a slightly tapering neck, and a fitted lid. Before you use the pot for the first time, fill it with hot water and set aside for 1 hour. Pour out the water and the pot is ready.

COFFEE, GREEK
This dark, rich coffee is brewed from powder-fine dark-roasted beans. It's made in a small, long-handled brass or tin pot *(briki)*, sweetened to taste, and served in tiny, straight-sided cups *(flintzania)*. Look for Greek (or Turkish) vacuum-packed coffee, coffeepots, and coffee cups in Greek and Middle Eastern stores. For a larger serving of coffee, use espresso or demitasse cups.

MAKING GREEK COFFEE
To a Greek or Turkish coffeepot, add 1 heaping teaspoon powder-fine ground coffee per *flintzani*-size cup of water (for a demitasse size, use 1½ heaping teaspoons). (Don't plan to fill the pot more than half full.) Add 1 teaspoon sugar or more to taste per serving. Add the correct amount of water to the pot and stir to dissolve the sugar. Place the pot over medium-high heat and heat until the foam reaches the top of the pot. Immediately pour into cups, filling them half full, then top each with some of the foam.

CURRANTS, DRIED
Named for the ancient city of Corinth, dried currants have played a role in meze table sauces and onion dishes for thousands of years. They are highly nutritious, and their sharp, tangy flavor is an effective appetite stimulator. Most imported Greek currants are sun-dried, but those from other sources may be sprayed, so check before buying. Store in a tightly covered jar in the pantry.

DOLMADES, DOLMADAKIA
Small parcels of grape leaf concealing a filling of rice and herbs, sometimes with the addition of nuts, spices, and/or meat. In winter, cabbage leaves are substituted for grape leaves; in early spring the daintiest dolmades are made with zucchini blossoms. Tiny dolmades for the meze table are called dolmadakia.

FAVA BEANS
This is the "bean of Greece," a source of protein in the Greek diet for over two millennia. Fresh beans are cooked whole in their pods for salads and casseroles, or eaten raw as an appetizer. Shelled young fava beans are also eaten skin-on, but more mature ones should be skinned: Blanch shelled favas in a medium saucepan of boiling water for 2 minutes. Drain, pull off the skin, and pop out the jade-green bean. Choose fava beans with care, discarding any blemished pods. Their fragile flavor harmonizes perfectly with olive oil, fresh herbs, and the flavors of a Greek spring: artichokes, wild greens, fresh cheese, and olives. Large favas are dried, to use later in the year as a puréed salad or a side dish.

FETA
see CHEESES.

FIGS
The fig tree, a native of Asia Minor, was appreciated throughout the ancient world and credited with miraculous life-sustaining properties. The fig has a unique botanical arrangement: What we think of as the fruit is a fleshy, vase-shaped sac; tiny flowers bloom inside it and the seeds are the real fruits. Common figs in the States include juicy amber-green Calimyrnas and Black Mission figs. Choose ripe figs, handle with care, and store in the refrigerator for only 1 or 2 days, remembering to move them to room temperature well in advance of serving to bring out their fullest flavor. Dried figs should be plump and moist; look for unsprayed Attica figs from Greece and Calimyrna figs from California.

FILO
These very thin pastry sheets (the word means "leaves" in Greek) are used to make some of the most delicate dishes on the meze table. Buy fresh or frozen filo from a good grocery store. Have the filling ready when you remove the pastry from the refrigerator, and work quickly and carefully. Filo contains little or no oil, so it's important to keep it moist; if it dries out it will be impossible to manipulate. Cover the filo first with plastic wrap, then with a damp kitchen towel. Always transfer frozen filo from the freezer to the refrigerator the day before you plan to use it, to allow it to thaw slowly.

GARBANZO BEANS (CHICKPEAS)
These small, yellow-ochre dried beans were first grown as a crop in ancient Egypt. Use wooden or other nonmetallic utensils with garbanzos if you can; metal utensils may produce an unpleasant flavor. Buy them in Greek, Middle Eastern, and natural foods stores; for the best-quality beans, look for a store with a fast turnover.

GARBANZO BEAN FLOUR (CHICKPEA FLOUR)
A fine, pale-yellow flour with a lingering, nutty flavor; look for it in natural foods stores, or in Greek, Middle Eastern, or Indian stores.

GARLIC
Whole garlic, raw or cooked, has a subtle aroma. Slicing strengthens flavor and aroma, chopping intensifies them, and crushing produces an assertive pungency. Traditional meze dishes work with this chemistry: In some, gentle cooking in olive oil subdues garlic's forceful character, while others exploit its natural exuberance to the full. For a few short weeks in spring, look for green garlic. Mild flavored and similar in appearance to green onions, it's delicious in meze salads or as a garnish. Or, grow your own and harvest the green shoots.

GRAPE LEAVES
Grape leaves are wrapped around or laid over grilled or baked foods to protect against fierce heat and to impart a lemony astringency; they are also folded over a spiced or herbal rice/meat filling to make bite-sized parcels (dolmades) for the meze table. The choicest dolmades are made with the tiniest, most tender leaves from the top third of the vine, and are a seasonal delicacy from mid-May through

early June. For the rest of the year, small grape leaves preserved in brine are used. Older leaves are used as an impromptu lid for baked vegetables and fish or as a wrapping for grilled foods, and are then discarded after cooking.

PREPARING FRESH GRAPE LEAVES
Trim each stem to ⅛ inch with a small pair of scissors. Dip the leaves, 4 or 5 at a time, in boiling water until they change color and become limp (about 4 seconds). Drain between paper towels.

PREPARING PRESERVED GRAPE LEAVES
Drain and soak the leaves for 10 minutes in cold water, changing the water 2 or 3 times. Or, rinse under cold running water, then dip briefly in boiling water.

GRAVIERA
see CHEESES.

GREENS
see KHORTA.

HERBS AND SPICES
Many of our best-loved herbs are native to Greece and the Eastern Mediterranean; they are easy to grow in pots or in the kitchen garden (for mail-order seeds, see Resources). Other herbs and spices here are widely available in good groceries, or in natural foods, Greek, or Middle Eastern stores.

BASIL
Pots of fragrant basil are a common sight in windows in Greece, as it is thought to keep away flies and mosquitoes, but the herb is only rarely used in cooking.

BAY LEAF (LAUREL)
Pungent and strong, bay leaf is an indispensable flavoring on the meze table. In Greece, dried figs are threaded on strings with bay leaves between them to keep flies at bay; before refrigeration, bay leaves were used to cover fish and meat while the barbecue or oven was prepared. A few bay leaves tied together make a perfect basting brush for grilled foods.

CILANTRO (FRESH CORIANDER)
Cultivated in Greece since antiquity, cilantro is a popular flavoring in meze dishes, especially those of dried beans or pork. Coriander seeds are dried and ground, and used to flavor chicken and beef.

CINNAMON
This heady spice lends an intriguing flavor to lamb or mushroom dishes. Whole cinnamon sticks can be stored almost indefinitely; ground cinnamon quickly loses its pungency, so buy only a little at a time.

CUMIN SEEDS
Cumin is a member of the same botanical family as dill, fennel, and cilantro. For the best flavor, buy the seeds whole and roast and grind them yourself when needed (see page 125).

DILL
In spring, the dark green fronds of fresh dill are a favorite flavoring in fresh bean dishes; dill is also used for shellfish and dried bean salata.

FENNEL
The silky, emerald-green fronds of fresh fennel flavor salads, khorta, pork dishes, pies, and beets. Young fennel shoots make an exquisite bread, and the seeds flavor liquor.

GERANIUM, LEMON- OR ROSE-SCENTED
These fragrant leaves are used to line storage containers for candies or fresh cheese; they are not eaten.

GREEK OREGANO (RIGANI)
The most favored meze herb is Greek oregano *(Origanum heracleoticum)*. Its tiny, sweetly perfumed pale-blue flowers are highly valued on the meze table, and the pungent oil of the dried leaves flavors many meze sauces. It's easy to mistake the more common oregano *(Origanum vulgare)* for this delicate herb, but it has a less refined, more acrid, flavor. It's well worth searching for bunches of dried Greek oregano (or rigani) in Greek and specialty foods stores. Or, substitute regular dried oregano.

LOVAGE
Similar in appearance and taste to wild celery, lovage grows wild in the steep ravines of Greece. Its crisp, fleshy stalks add zest to soups and casseroles and are used to flavor dishes of boiled greens or dried beans.

MARJORAM
Pot marjoram *(Origanum onites),* a smaller, more delicate herb than sweet marjoram *(Origanum hortensis),* is the preferred herb in meze cooking. Fresh or dried marjoram is the perfect partner to lamb, and a favorite ingredient in dishes using red wine vinegar.

MINT
Several varieties of mint are used in meze cooking: Spearmint flavors yogurt dishes; water mint is the preferred mint to use in stuffed vegetables. Other mints—lemon mint, peppermint, corn mint—are used to make herbal teas.

PARSLEY
Rich in vitamins and minerals, fresh flat-leaf parsley is used with abandon on the meze table. Greeks regard parsley as a true tonic—it stimulates the digestive system and encourages appetite. Take a minute or two to strip leaves from stalks, to prevent any trace of bitterness in your finished dish.

PEPPER
Pungent black pepper plays an important role on the meze table; it enlivens taste buds and stimulates appetite. There is no substitute for freshly ground pepper, so it's worth investing in a pepper mill. Some meze dishes call for the added refinement of finely cracked pepper; use the largest grind on your pepper

mill or spread the peppercorns under waxed paper and crush with a rolling pin.

ROSEMARY
In Greece, the best rosemary is said to grow on dry hills close to the sea, so it's not surprising to find its clean, clear perfume in fish mezes. The small, firm branches are also used as basting brushes for grilled meat, kephtedes, and fish.

SAGE
The intoxicating, elusive aroma of sage has a valued place on the summer meze grill. Its young, fresh leaves impart their musky, pinelike flavor to chicken and game. Dried sage can be substituted for fresh, but use half the quantity called for in a recipe.

SUMAC
This ground spice gives a wonderful tangy flavor to grills and salads. Sumac berries are harvested in late summer and dried on the branch, then ground into a coarse, deep-red powder. Since the quality of sumac can vary, buy it from a reputable market and store in the refrigerator or freezer (see Resources). Paprika can be substituted for sumac, but sprinkle a squeeze of fresh lemon juice over the dish, too.

THYME
For the table, Greek village cooks grow thyme in pots, in their shady courtyards; the thyme that blankets the mountain foothills is too strong to use in cooking. But this wild herb lends its lovely fragrance to the meze table in another way: It provides food for the goats and sheep, and nectar for the bees.

WINTER SAVORY
With its sharp, peppery flavor, and at its most prolific in spring, winter savory is a natural partner to early-season carrots and fava beans, and a good choice to flavor Yogurt Cheese (page 18).

HONEY
The ancients used honey as a preservative and in marinades, and it is still valued as an instant energizer, packed with vitamins and minerals and, some say, a mysterious and beneficial X factor. Thyme-blossom honey from Mount Hymettus, one of the best Greek honeys, is available in Greek and Middle Eastern stores, or substitute another full-flavored honey like orange-blossom honey.

KASSERI
see CHEESES.

KEPHALOTYRI
see CHEESES.

KEPHTEDES, KEPHTEDAKIA
Highly flavored grilled, fried, or poached patties of meat, chicken, game, fish, or vegetables. They can be round, oblong, or square, and may vary in size from tiny (kephtedakia), for a dainty meze, to main-course size (kephtedes). In style and flavor, kephtedes are unchanged since antiquity.

KHORTA
The generic name for a host of edible wild greens that flourish after the first fall rains and for which Greeks have a passion. In early fall, zucchini shoots and wild mustard (*sinapi*) are collected; through fall, winter, and early spring, there are wild beet greens (*vlita*), charlock (*vrouves*), eryngo shoots (*sfalangatho*), dandelion (*agriorathiki*), black nightshade (*stifnos*), mallow (*mochles*), centaura (*alivarvara*), and burdock (*lappato*). Spring is the season for wild chicory (*radiki*), wild asparagus, lamb's-quarter (*agriospanakia*), and pea shoots (*papoules*); special delicacies are the young leaves of the Spanish oyster plant (*askolimvros*), grape hyacinth leaves, and wild garlic. The first small, tender leaves of khorta are eaten raw, in green salads; older, or larger, leaves are cooked and served warm or at room temperature with a dressing of olive oil and red wine vinegar or lemon juice. In the States, many of these greens are grown commercially, such as mustard greens, dandelion greens, beet greens, broccoli rabe, amaranth greens, and chard.

PREPARING AND COOKING GREENS
Discard the stalks and tear large leaves into smaller pieces. In a large nonreactive saucepan, bring ½ cup water to a boil. Add the greens and cover. Reduce heat to low and cook tender chard, beet, zucchini, or dandelion greens for 1 to 2 minutes, turnip greens for 3 to 4 minutes, and amaranth or mustard for about 5 minutes, or until wilted and tender. Drain in a colander, pressing on the greens with the back of a large wooden spoon to release the moisture.

LAKERTHA
see BONITO.

LENTILS
Both green and brown lentils are used in Greek cooking; look for them in Greek, Middle Eastern, or natural foods stores.

COOKING LENTILS
Rinse and pick over the lentils. Put the lentils in a saucepan, add water to cover by 2 inches, and bring to a boil over medium-low heat. Reduce heat to low, cover, and simmer for 15 to 20 minutes, or until just tender; drain.

LOVAGE
see HERBS AND SPICES.

MANOURI
see CHEESES.

MAVRODAPHNE
see WINES AND SPIRITS.

MUSCOVADO SUGAR
A dark brown, richly flavored cane sugar; substitute Hymettus or other strong honey.

MUSTARD, PREPARED

The fiery mustard condiment on our tables is unknown in traditional Greek cooking. In Cretan village kitchens, a very mild condiment is made from the seeds of wild mustard greens; its nearest taste equivalent is Meaux mustard from France *(moutarde de Meaux)*. As a substitute for 1 tablespoon Meaux mustard, use ½ tablespoon Dijon mustard mixed with 1 teaspoon of honey.

OCTOPUS

Usually sold cleaned and tenderized, octopus must be skinned before being turned into a meze. Smoked or sun-dried octopus, available in good Greek or Middle Eastern stores, makes tasty and unusual appetizers.

OKRA

A member of the mallow family brought to Greece by early Egyptian traders, okra has a slightly acidic flavor well suited to the summer meze table. For Greek okra dishes, the pods are used whole; don't pierce the pods or they will burst, releasing gelatinous juices and giving the dish a gumbolike texture that is unknown in Greek cooking.

OLIVE OIL

The health-enhancing properties of olive oil are now widely recognized, and Greek olive oil, produced in the country for over three thousand years, is finally attracting the attention it deserves. Greek extra-virgin olive oil finds its perfect role on the meze table—for flavoring, preserving, moistening, and cooking—and there is no substitute for its rich, glossy beauty. The best (from Crete or the Peloponnese, or kalamata extra-virgin olive oil) are distinguished by a rich, heady flavor and a mildly fruity aroma. Buy young oils with a fruity, recognizable taste and a good balance of flavors.

OLIVES

Relatively few types of olives are grown in Greece, but there is a huge range of cured olives. Olives are named for their place of origin (Kalamata, Amfissa, Atalanti, Nafplion, Volos), their color (black, purple, green), or their method of curing (brining or salt-curing). Greek olives are some of the best available, because a number of producers still use traditional methods of harvesting and curing. Most of the following olives can be found in Greek stores or good grocery stores, or you can order them (see Resources).

AMFISSA

Large, black, and mellow-flavored, these olives are good with vegetable mezes and country bread.

ATALANTI

Plump, fleshy, and brine-cured, purple or purple-green Atalanti are fruity and luscious, with an exquisite flavor and a texture that blends beautifully with grilled meats.

ELITSES

From Crete, these tiny purple-brown olives have a gentle, almost sweet, flavor. If you can't find them, substitute niçoise olives from France.

IONIAN

These large, plump, fresh-tasting green olives are the perfect complement to the spring flavors of artichokes or asparagus and retsina wine.

KALAMATA

Glossy purple-black, almond-shaped kalamatas are probably the best-known Greek olives. They are an excellent foil for strong meze flavors like feta cheese and oregano-perfumed grills, or for ripe tomatoes and purées of dried beans.

KHOURMADES (LITERALLY, "DATES")

These large, wrinkled, dark brown olives from the island of Chios are good with goat cheese.

NAFPLION

Green olives from the eastern Peloponnese, these marry well with the strong flavors of preserved fish—try them with taramosalata (puréed mullet roe) or with salted anchovies or sardines.

THASOS

Black, chewy, salt-cured olives with a wrinkly skin and intense flavor. Like throumbes, below, these are good partners for sun-dried or smoked fish and meat, pulse dishes, and fresh or aged sheep cheese.

THROUMBES

These are the small, meaty, tree-ripened brown-black olives that are served in every village café.

TSATSIKES

These cracked "green country" olives are very good with fresh sheep cheese, bread, and a glass of ouzo.

ORANGE-FLOWER WATER

Distilled from bitter-orange blossoms and used to flavor desserts and other foods. Available from Greek, Middle Eastern, or natural foods stores.

OUZO

see WINES AND SPIRITS.

PASTOURMAS

This highly spiced preserved meat, especially veal or pork, is available in the central markets of Thessaloniki and Athens but difficult to find outside Greece. Speck ham, from Switzerland, or prosciutto are good substitutes.

PEA SHOOTS

The tender greens from the tips of the pea vine. They are picked until the pea pods form; after this, the greens develop a slightly bitter taste.

PEPPERS

Roasted and peeled sweet red bell peppers are used in many Greek dishes. Although they are available in jars, it's best to make your own.

ROASTING AND PEELING PEPPERS

Grill whole over charcoal or an open flame, or cut in half lengthwise and place under a broiler, until evenly charred. Put the peppers in a paper or plastic bag, seal the bag, and let sit until cool to the touch. With your fingers, rub off the skins. Remove and discard the seeds and ribs.

PINE NUTS

The cones of the stone pine trees along the Greek coastline can be harvested only every three years, and the nuts must be removed from the cones by hand. Consequently, pine nuts are expensive, even in Greece. The best available *(Pinus pinea)* are imported from the Mediterranean. Buy them in small quantities and store in an airtight container in a dark, cool place, or freeze.

TOASTING PINE NUTS
Lightly brush a jellyroll pan with olive oil and spread the pine nuts in a single layer. Bake in a preheated 300°F oven for 10 minutes, or until toasted, shaking the pan occasionally.

PISTACHIO NUTS

A rich source of nutrients (especially potassium), pistachio nuts will keep several months in a tightly sealed container. Traditionally, the best Greek pistachios are from the island of Aegina, where islanders tie pistachio-packed sacks to large rocks just beneath the tide line. As the sacks gently roll in the sea wash, the nuts rub together and the friction strips off their soft outer fruit to expose the nuts within. In September, these fresh pistachios are sold on every Athens street corner. For the best flavor, buy unsalted pistachios (see Resources).

POMEGRANATE MOLASSES

Look for this condiment in Middle Eastern stores under its Arab name, *rebb el-rumman*. It is made by boiling fresh pomegranate juice until it reduces to a brownish-red liquid. If you have a pomegranate tree, it is easy to do this yourself; use a nonreactive pan and store in small quantities in the freezer. Pomegranate molasses gives a delicious sweet-sour flavor to sauces and stuffings.

PRESERVED LEMONS

Preserving lemons softens and mellows the rinds so they can be eaten and used to flavor stews and many other dishes.

MAKING PRESERVED LEMONS
Wash 4 small organic lemons and sterilize a 1-pint glass or earthenware jar. Cut off and discard a thin slice from both ends of 3 of the lemons and cut the lemons into ¼-inch-thick slices; reserve any juice. Flick out the seeds with the point of a small knife. Arrange a layer of one-fourth of the lemon slices in the jar. Sprinkle with 1 scant teaspoon coarse sea salt, ½ teaspoon coriander seeds, and a bay leaf. Repeat 3 times. Juice the remaining lemon and pour this over the lemon slices, along with any reserved juice. Cover with 2 layers of cheesecloth and carefully shake the jar to distribute the salt. Set aside in the sun or on a shelf for 2 days; shake the jar once or twice during this time. Taste the brine: If it has lost its original harsh flavor, it's ready; if not, leave a day or two longer in the same spot. Add about 1 cup olive oil or more as needed to cover the lemons and tightly cover the jar with plastic wrap or 2 layers of waxed paper secured under a lid. Store at room temperature for 2 weeks to 3 months. Makes 1 pint.

PULSES

"Old world" beans—garbanzos, favas, split peas, and lentils—have been excavated in Minoan and Classical archaeological sites throughout Greece and her islands. For today's Greek family, dried bean dishes are comforting fare during winter and religious fasts, and bean-based mezes appear on domestic and taverna tables throughout the year.

COOKING DRIED BEANS
Rinse and pick over the beans. Soak in water to cover by 2 inches overnight; drain. Put the beans in a large saucepan with cold water to cover. Bring to a boil, simmer for 10 minutes, then drain; rinse both beans and pan. Return the beans to the saucepan and add cold water to cover by at least 4 inches. Bring to a boil, reduce heat, cover, and simmer until tender. Don't add salt or acidic ingredients such as tomatoes or lemon juice until the end of the cooking time, as acid can inhibit the cooking process.

PURSLANE

The earthy flavor and crunchy texture of purslane make it a good foil for vegetables such as potatoes, beets, or fava beans, a perfect garnish for grilled fish, and a unique ingredient in green salads. Purslane is easy to grow at home (for seed sources, see Resources).

QUINCES

In Greek legend, the quince is a native of Crete, named for the town of Kydonia, now known as Chania. Associated with the goddess Aphrodite, it has come to symbolize love and fertility. In the fall, Cretan markets boast magnificent displays of golden yellow just-ripe quinces the size of large grapefruit and with a heavenly scent.

Quinces grow well in California and in parts of New York state and the Southwest, and can be found in season in farmers' markets in those areas. Choose firm, pale-yellow fruit for best texture and flavor. If only underripe greenish-yellow fruits are available, use them to make Quince Candies (page 34). Be aware that raw quinces do not make pleasant eating. Underripe quinces can be kept a month or two—just wipe off their fuzzy down and store them, stem down, in a single layer and separated from each other, on slatted shelves in a well-ventilated cupboard.

PREPARING QUINCES
Blanch them in boiling water for 1 minute, then use a stainless-steel knife to peel, core, and slice.

RAKI
see WINES AND SPIRITS, TSIPOURO.

RETSINA
see WINES AND SPIRITS, TSIPOURO.

RIGANI, DRIED
see GREEK OREGANO.

ROMAINE LETTUCE
Originally named for the island of Kos, where these juicy, tender lettuces were said to have been grown by the gardeners of antiquity to heights of 3 or 4 feet. In later centuries, when the lettuce became popular in Italy and France, it was renamed romaine (Roman), though it is still known as Kos lettuce in Greece.

SALAD GREENS
There is now a developing appreciation of the astringent flavor and nutritional value of a variety of salad greens. Young beet leaves, turnip or radish tops, and many other bitter greens, including frisée (closest in flavor to Greece's wild greens, see KHORTA) and dandelion greens, are available in ethnic and specialty markets. Buy only young, very fresh greens and use quickly. Mixed salad greens, a combination of mild and bitter leaves of baby lettuce and baby greens, is found in many specialty foods stores.

SALATA
Literally, the word means "salad," but Greek salads (salates) are not always what we expect them to be. Many are purées, others are vegetable salads. Green salads are called *salatika*.

SAMOS NECTAR
see WINES AND SPIRITS.

SAMPHIRE
This plant grows wild on sea-facing cliffs and is at its best in late spring and early summer, when its shoots and fronds are a bright emerald green. Samphire *(Crithium maritimum)* belongs to the same botanical family as celery and fennel. You need only to rinse young samphire before using, but older samphire should be blanched for 30 seconds in boiling water, drained, and patted dry.

SEA SALT
A digestive and an appetizer, sea salt balances and mellows flavors. Use fine salt in cooking, or add coarse salt to dishes before serving.

SEA URCHINS
The coral roe of sea urchins *(achinoi)* has been a delicacy since the days of Homer. Female sea urchins are traditionally gathered during the nights of the full moon, when they supposedly contain the greatest number of eggs. Sea urchins are hugely popular in Greece (perhaps because Cretan folklore proclaims them to be a powerful aphrodisiac), and beach and harborside vendors sell them from huge baskets, cracking them open for customers to eat on the spot.

Sea urchins, which are bought live and eaten raw, can occasionally be found in the fish markets of New York, San Francisco, and Los Angeles. Buy very fresh sea urchins from a reputable supplier and prepare them yourself. At home, store them for no longer than 4 hours, in a basket lined with a damp tea towel and covered with another damp towel; refrigerate in warm weather.

PREPARING SEA URCHINS
Cover one hand with a heavy cloth and use it to grip one sea urchin, beak upwards. With a narrow, blunt-ended knife, cut into the exposed soft part and gently maneuver the knife to scoop out this and the top third of the shell. Have a bucket of clean water at your side and, as you finish each urchin, rinse out the loose gray inner mass and any broken spines, leaving the roe adhering to the shell in a five-pointed star.

Serve sea urchins in the shell so guests can scoop out the roe for themselves. Allow 2 or 3 per person, and serve with bread and lemon wedges. Or, scoop out the roe onto a small platter and sprinkle with a few drops of fresh lemon juice and extra-virgin olive oil. Serve immediately, or tightly cover with plastic wrap and refrigerate for no longer than 1 hour.

SEEDS
Seeds have been an important source of protein and minerals for Greeks since ancient times. Sesame seeds flavor meze vegetable dishes; dried melon, sunflower, and pumpkin seeds are served as "nibbles" to accompany a glass of ouzo or tsipouro. Look for these seeds in Greek, Middle Eastern, or natural foods stores. Or, on a hot, sunny day, dry your own melon or pumpkin seeds: Remove the seeds from the fruit and rinse off all traces of fiber; drain and spread on paper towels to dry. Spread them in one layer on a baking sheet, cover with cheesecloth, and leave for 1 day in a shady spot outside; shake the pan occasionally.

TOASTING SEEDS
Spread seeds in one layer on a baking sheet. Toast in a preheated 325°F oven for about 6 minutes, or until lightly fragrant; shake the pan once or twice.

SFONGATA SKILLETS
The museums of Athens offer fascinating glimpses into the culinary past, including ancient sfongata skillets. Today, this pan is still produced along the same traditional lines. Made of cast iron, the sfongata skillet has rounded sloping sides and two handles, and is about 2 inches deep. Sfongata can also be made in an omelet pan (a 10-inch pan makes an 8-portion sfongata) or a regular cast-iron skillet.

SOUVLAKIA
These skewers of lean meat or firm-fleshed fish, dipped in a flavorful marinade and grilled over charcoal, derive their name from *souvla*, the Greek word for a metal rod, or spit. They are said to have been introduced by Greek gourmets of antiquity who disdained the contemporary European practice of tearing at a carcass with the hands!

SQUID (KALAMARIA)

A favorite late-spring and summer food in Greece and widely available in the United States. Fresh squid is firm and shiny, with a lightly mottled pink skin. For the meze table, fry tiny whole squid; cut larger ones in strips and grill.

CLEANING SQUID

Gently pull the head from the body and cut off the two attached fins. Discard the body contents (use your finger, or slit the bag from end to end, to check) but set aside the ink sac for use later in pasta sauces. Cut off and discard the strip containing the eyes and press out the tough beak. Thoroughly rinse the squid, rubbing both tentacles and body with your fingers to remove any sand or tough skin.

SUMAC

see HERBS AND SPICES.

TAHINI

This sesame-seed paste can be found in Greek, Middle Eastern, and natural foods stores. It doesn't need to be refrigerated, but it will separate into a very thick paste with a surface layer of oil if left more than a day or two; before measuring for a recipe, stir well.

TOMATOES

You can almost taste the sun in Greek tomatoes, especially those from Crete, an island that enjoys 360 days of sunshine each year. Kos islanders produce wonderful sun-dried tomatoes with a concentrated natural sweetness for use in aromatic meze dishes, while the fertile volcanic soil of Santorini produces tiny, intensely sweet deep-red tomatoes.

We can improve the flavor of the tomatoes available to us by exaggerating the tomato's sweetness for meze dishes. A little honey or sugar added to cooking tomatoes converts the natural acid to sweetness, while a pinch of sugar inside tomato shells to be used for stuffing greatly improves their flavor. For an exqui-site tomato salad, slice the tomatoes 1 hour before serving, sprinkle with superfine sugar (½ teaspoon to 1 pound tomatoes) and sea salt to taste, cover lightly, and set aside in a cool spot (not the refrigerator). To serve, pour over extra-virgin olive oil and sprinkle with freshly milled black pepper, a few olives, and a little crumbled feta cheese.

PEELING AND SEEDING TOMATOES

Add tomatoes, a few at a time, to a saucepan of simmering water and leave 10 to 30 seconds; as the skin of each one splits, remove with a slotted spoon. When cool to the touch, peel off the skin. To seed, cut a tomato crosswise in half and gently squeeze out the seeds.

TSIPOURO

see WINES AND SPIRITS.

VINEGAR

The tang of red wine vinegar is an essential meze table taste, and Greek cooks have a traditional understanding of its use as a subtle flavoring. Two main techniques are used in meze dishes: cooking vinegar to reduce it, or using a small quantity to finish a dish. The vinegar of choice for meze dishes is aged red wine vinegar, available in good grocery stores. In cooked mezes, you can substitute the stronger, more pungent balsamic vinegar; for 2 tablespoons red wine vinegar, use 1 tablespoon balsamic vinegar combined with 1 tablespoon water.

WALNUT OIL

You can find this in specialty food stores and good natural foods stores. Look for a fresh oil (one less than 1 year old) and store in a tightly sealed container away from sunlight.

WALNUTS

Long the most popular nut in Greek cooking, walnuts are served with a glass of ouzo or raki or drenched in thick honey as a sweetmeat. Young walnuts, still in their soft shells, are preserved for the winter in salt and vinegar for savory mezes, or in honey, to enjoy with liqueurs. Walnuts are used in cakes and sprinkled over desserts, distilled into a liqueur, and pounded into a sauce (page 110); older villagers still make a traditional rich walnut oil to flavor potato and dried-bean mezes. Freshly gathered walnuts have the richest oil and flavor, so buy only from the current year's crop.

WILD GREENS

see KHORTA.

WINES AND SPIRITS

The meze table is no place for complex wines or fancy cocktails—the flavors of the foods take center stage. For excitement and value, look for Greek wines labeled *Table Wine* or *Vin de Pays*, especially if they are made from indigenous Greek grapes. There has been a magnificent renaissance in Greek wine making in the last 15 years, and it's well worth searching for the wines. For an unusual "taste of Greece" try one of the very good Greek rosé wines; look for those from Kourtakis, Semeli, Skouras, Strofilia, and Tsantsalis.

MAVRODAPHNE

A portlike dessert wine that's produced near Patras. The name means "black laurel." Port, Malmsey, or Madeira can be substituted.

OUZO

This potent anise-flavored liquor is distilled from the remnants of pressed grapes. In Greece, it is served straight, in a shot glass, accompanied with a tall glass of cold water. (Serving ouzo over ice is a modern innovation.) Serve with fish and grilled-meat mezes, especially those flavored with lemon juice. Look for *Ouzo Athenée, Tsantsalis' Olympic,* and *Babatzim's Ouzo.*

RETSINA

This unusual wine has a wonderful affinity with open-air food and is the traditional drink of spring and summer tables. It's distinctive flavor is thought to owe its origins to the Attica region, where the wine producers of antiquity may have used equipment made from local pine wood or heat sealed their storage jars with resin pitch. Today, Greece holds the only international appellation for resinated wine, and although some independent producers still store retsina in pitch-sealed barrels, most commercial producers add resin during fermentation.

The Savatiano grape produces an aromatic retsina with a fresh, dry flavor, a light gold color, and a soft pine taste. It should be served nicely chilled. Look for retsinas labeled *Kourtakis, Tsantalis, Boutari,* or the *Thebes Wine Cooperative.* Look also for *Kokkineli,* an antique rosé version made with the roditis grape.

SAMOS NECTAR
This is a honey-gold, gently sweet Muscat produced on the island of Samos. Look for the *Kourtakis* label here.

TSIPOURO (OR *RAKI* OR *TSIGOUITHIA*)
At its best, this is a strong, smooth distillate with a clean, fiery taste. Very little is exported but, if you can find tsipouro, it's the best drink to serve with vinegar-flavored mezes. Try tsipouro from *Babatzim, Ktima Lazaridi, Parparoussis,* and *Averoff.*

ZEST
Use only the colored zest of citrus fruits, which is easy to remove with a zester (you can find this inexpensive little instrument in good hardware stores). If you suspect that your fruit may have been sprayed with pesticides, blanch the zest in boiling water for 1 minute, then rinse under cold running water.

ⓔⓧⓔⓧ

RESOURCES

If you can't locate some of the ingredients used in these recipes, try the following Web sites and mail-order sources.

PANTRY INGREDIENTS
thegreekconnection.com

esperya.com

gourmetresource.com

deandeluca.com

OLIVES AND OLIVE OIL
blauel.gr

greekartisans.com

minerva.com

CHEESES
cowgirlcreamery.com

mtvikos.com

rockridgemarkethall.com

worldofcheese.com

zingermans.com

WINES
greekwineguide.gr

geowine.gr

museum.upenn.edu/favorite wine

nestorimports.com

SEEDS
futurefoods.com

The Cook's Garden Catalog 800.457.9703

Johnny's Selected Seeds 800.437.4301

INDEX

TABLE OF EQUIVALENTS

The exact equivalents in the following tables have been rounded for convenience.

LIQUID/ DRY MEASURES

U.S.	METRIC
¼ teaspoon	1.25 milliliters
½ teaspoon	2.5 milliliters
1 teaspoon	5 milliliters
1 tablespoon (3 teaspoons)	15 milliliters
1 fluid ounce (2 tablespoons)	30 milliliters
¼ cup	60 milliliters
⅓ cup	80 milliliters
½ cup	120 milliliters
1 cup	240 milliliters
1 pint (2 cups)	480 milliliters
1 quart (4 cups, 32 ounces)	960 milliliters
1 gallon (4 quarts)	3.84 liters
1 ounce (by weight)	28 grams
1 pound	454 grams
2.2 pounds	1 kilogram

LENGTH

U.S.	METRIC
⅛ inch	3 millimeters
¼ inch	6 millimeters
½ inch	12 millimeters
1 inch	2.5 centimeters

OVEN TEMPERATURE

FAHRENHEIT	CELSIUS	GAS
250	120	½
275	140	1
300	150	2
325	160	3
350	180	4
375	190	5
400	200	6
425	220	7
450	230	8
475	240	9
500	260	10